IRREVOCABLY INTERTWINED

Analyzing the Plays of Edward Albee

Greg Carlisle

g.carlisle@moreheadstate.edu

IRREVOCABLY

INTERTWINED

Analyzing the Plays
of Edward Albee

GREG CARLISLE

SSMG PRESS / LOS ANGELES

Irrevocably Intertwined
Analyzing the Plays of Edward Albee
Greg Carlisle

SSMG Press
Sideshow Media Group
8033 Sunset Blvd. #164
Los Angeles, CA. 90046
USA
sideshowmediagroup.com
Cover Design by Kyle Ware

Contents

for my wife and daughters

ACKNOWLEDGEMENTS

I count the enduring support and encouragement of Matt Bucher and John Bucher and my near-quarter-century friendship with Kyle Ware as three of my greatest blessings. Thanks to all of you for your interest and faith in my work.

INTRODUCTION

This book takes a brief look at the structural integrity of each of Edward Albee's published plays and also calls attention to Albee's consistency and unflinching honesty across a body of work that spans over fifty years. Considered as a whole, Albee's plays have a thematic unity that puts his artistic project into sharp focus. And though Albee crafts each individual play to suit its content, there are dramaturgical techniques that recur across his varied plays. Early in his career, Albee was linked with a group of playwrights who were creating a Theatre of the Absurd as defined by Martin Esslin in 1961. While Absurdism is not usually the best lens through which to view Albee's work, "the absurd is the lens through which many people encounter Albee" (Bennett *EAA* 2), and the primary concerns of the Theatre of the Absurd articulated by Esslin are essentially Albee's concerns as well. But as Michael Y. Bennett states in his introduction to *Edward Albee and Absurdism*, the inaugural volume of *New Perspectives in Edward Albee Studies*, discussions of Albee's work "should not be limited to *only* absurdism"

(2), because the "absurd affiliation often precipitates a glossing over of the variegated and complex themes and experiments that can be found in Albee's decades-long career" (1). By confronting "the 'absurd' label that has so often stuck to the plays of Edward Albee" Bennett hopes to inspire Albee scholars to "move on" and "investigate a number of more pertinent ideas, subjects, and issues related to and found in Albee's *oeuvre*" (2). Although this book initiates a discussion of the recurring themes in Albee's work by grounding them in Absurdist thought, it is also my hope that this book will inspire conversations about Albee's work to move in other directions.

Albee defended the Theatre of the Absurd in a 1962 essay, citing Esslin's summation of the Theatre of the Absurd as an attempt to make modern man "face up to the human condition as it really is, to free him from illusions that are bound to cause constant maladjustment and disappointment...For the dignity of man lies in his ability to face reality in all its senselessness; to accept it freely, without fear, without illusions—and to laugh at it" (*SMM* 9, Esslin 428-9). The Theatre of the Absurd "fulfils a dual purpose" in Esslin's construct. First, "it castigates, satirically, the absurdity of lives lived unaware and unconscious of ultimate reality," the "deadness and mechanical senselessness of half-unconscious lives" (Esslin 400). Discussing his play *Seascape* in the mid-1970s, Albee said that "People closing down, how people get along with one another, how they make a marriage" were "matters that concerned him in all his plays" (Gussow 289). In 1991 Albee said, "All my plays are about people missing the boat, closing down too young, coming to the end of their lives with regret at things not done, as opposed to things done" (Gussow 359). More significantly and positively, the second purpose of the Theatre of the Absurd is to assert that "life must be faced in its ultimate, stark reality." "[S]tripped of the accidental circumstances of social position or historical context," man must confront "the basic choices, the basic situations of his existence." Esslin provides eight examples of those basic situations and asserts that their common feature is the inability of man "to reach his fellow man" (Esslin 401-2). Albee strips his characters of "the veneer we call civilization" (*Counting the Ways*, *2CP* 546) to make them aware that they are "irrevocably intertwined" (*Marriage Play*, *3CP* 304), struggling with their simultaneous desire and inability to reach each other. The need to break through our illusions and sense of isolation to an underlying truth or to an honest moment of communion with another person is at the heart of all of Albee's work.

While Albee's concerns align with these general purposes of the Theatre of the Absurd, Albee's work does not exemplify the more extreme characteristics of the Theatre of the Absurd outlined by Esslin: its difference in form from realistic theatre (Esslin 403), "its devaluation of language" (407) into nonsense, "a grotesquely heightened and distorted picture of a world that has gone mad" (410), and "characters whose motives and actions remain largely incomprehensible" (411). Rather than presenting the audience with "a picture of a disintegrating world" (411), Albee presents disintegrating relationships. However, there are some specific commonalities between Esslin's characterizations of the Theatre of the Absurd and Albee's dramaturgy: the restoration of language to "the expression of authentic content, rather than its concealment" (408-9), "circular structure" (415-6), "profoundly experienced emotion" (421), and "the living, recurring poetic imagery of ritual" (424). Albee's characters actively and consistently use language to clarify, to question, to challenge, and often to incant as well. Albee masterfully uses language musically and lays the blueprint for intense, emotionally charged rituals through the repetition of words as simple as "no" and "yes" (as in *The Play About the Baby, 3CP* 532-3). A few of Albee's plays are circular in the sense of "ending exactly as they began" (Esslin 416), but they are more likely to have what Albee calls a culminating center. Writing about his play *Fragments*, he says, "Dramatic shape need not be linear but could be a vortex, moving from all sides at once toward a culminating center" (*3CP* 8). Speaking of art, Voice in Albee's *Box* says, "No matter how far traveled, one comes back, not circular, not to the starting point, but a…setting down again, and the beauty of art is order—not what is familiar, necessarily, but order…on its own terms" (*2CP* 265).

In his 2001 reassessment of the Theatre of the Absurd, Bennett states:

> For Camus and Ionesco, the absurd was a *situation*, but not a life sentence of destined meaninglessness or a comment on the world. True, life *might* not have any inherent meaning, but this stems not from the world, but from the contradiction between our desires and what the world offers us. However, given the absurdity of this situation, it is up to us, through our defiance, revolt, and contemplation, to make our lives meaningful. (Bennett *RTA* 10)

In Albee's work, our absurd situation can be characterized as a contradiction or gap between our desires and what specific other people offer us, rather than what the world in general offers us. This gap between desire and offer underlies and gives coherence to Albee's thematic motifs, italicized below. Albee often equates our desires with *our animal natures*, and while that can mean desperate, self-focused need, it also means the need to bond with another or with a group.

But bonds with other desiring beings generate conflict, and most of Albee's plays explore *the strain of conflict on our marriage or family bonds*. The simultaneous, paradoxical need to be understood on our own terms while craving communion with others effects *the shaping of our identities*, so Albee's characters frequently ask "Who am I?" or even "Do I exist?" The inability to bridge the gap between our desires and what other people offer us creates an environment of anxiety and therefore fear, because the only certainties in life are loss and eventually a visceral understanding that we are dying. Albee's struggling characters are meant to inspire us to face *the reality of our losses, our fears, and our mortality*. The expression of loss in Albee's work is most palpable when the subject concerns *an absent or damaged child*. Thomas P. Adler also asserts that "there is a thematic coherence from play to play that imparts to [Albee's] body of work a unity of purpose and perspective" and has articulated a comparable set of thematic motifs in Albee's work (Adler 88). Toby Zinman documents Albee's "recurrent preoccupations" (Zinman 4-9). Readers of this book's play-by-play analysis of Albee's work are encouraged to consider Zinman's *Edward Albee* (2008) and Matthew Roudané's *Edward Albee: A Critical Introduction* (2017) as well.

Albee's insistence on awareness over illusion is expressed in his dramaturgy as well. In almost every play, his characters are keenly aware of their linguistic choices as they are making them, often altering the rhythm of their dialogue to comment on those choices. Many of his characters, especially in the later plays, speak to the audience with an intent to persuade that goes beyond the standard asides and narration of conventional audience address. By acknowledging the conventional trappings of theatrical art, Albee, like Brecht, invites audiences to move beyond passive enjoyment of an illusory entertainment to a more palpable state of engagement with the ideas and situations his characters present. These touches of meta-awareness contribute to our understanding of the plays as promoting profound contemplation and empathy rather than passivity and nihilism, giving us a more objective view of the often bleak circumstances in which Albee's characters are struggling. Albee also occasionally acknowledges his own place in a theatrical tradition by making references to other dramatic works, including his own. Albee engages his characters in witty games and powerful rituals that almost always lead to dark or unsettling truths

EDWARD ALBEE'S PLAYS	THEMATIC MOTIFS	Animal Nature	Marriage, Family Bond/Conflict	Identity: Who Am I? Do I Exist?	Face Reality: Loss, Fear, Dying	An Absent or Damaged Child	DRAMATURGICAL MOTIFS	Meta-awareness	Of Language	Of Audience	Of Theatrical Art	Verbal Virtuosity	Rituals, Games	Monologues	Characters	Multiple Pairs	Names Abstracted	Environment	Open	Confined	Structure	Climactic	Episodic	Culminating Center
The Zoo Story		x	x	x	x			x							x				x			x		x
The Death of Bessie Smith			x	x											x		x		x			x		
The Sandbox			x		x			x	x	x		x					x		x			x		
Fam and Yam			x								x						x			x		x		
The American Dream			x	x	x	x		x	x						x		x			x		x		
Who's Afraid of Virginia Woolf?		x	x	x	x	x		x		x		x	x	x			x			x		x		x
The Ballad of the Sad Café		x	x	x	x				x						x		x						x	
Tiny Alice		x		x	x			x				x	x			x	x	x		x		x		x
Malcolm			x	x	x	x		x				x	x	x			x		x				x	
A Delicate Balance			x		x	x		x		x			x	x			x		x					
Everything in the Garden			x	x	x			x	x	x				x			x		x					
Box and Quotations/Mao Tse-tung		x	x	x	x				x			x	x		x		x		x					x
All Over		x	x		x			x				x	x		x		x		x					
Seascape		x	x	x	x			x		x		x	x	x			x		x					
Listening		x		x	x	x			x			x	x		x		x		x					x
Counting the Ways		x	x		x			x	x	x		x	x		x		x					x	x	x
The Lady from Dubuque		x	x	x	x			x	x	x		x	x	x			x		x					
Lolita		x		x	x	x		x	x	x					x		x		x			x		
The Man Who Had Three Arms			x	x				x	x	x					x		x		x					
Finding the Sun		x	x	x	x	x		x	x	x		x	x		x	x	x		x					x
Marriage Play		x	x	x				x		x		x	x							x				x
Three Tall Women		x	x	x	x	x		x	x			x	x		x					x				x
Fragments		x		x	x	x		x	x	x					x		x		x					x
The Play About the Baby			x	x	x	x		x	x	x		x	x	x	x	x								x
The Goat, or Who Is Sylvia?		x	x	x	x			x		x		x	x						x			x		
Occupant			x	x	x			x	x	x			x		x		x							x
Knock! Knock! Who's There!?			x	x					x	x	x		x			x			x					x
At Home at the Zoo		x	x	x	x	x		x							x		x	x	x			x		x
Me, Myself & I			x	x	x			x	x	x					x		x		x			x		x

Figure 1. Thematic and Dramaturgical Motifs in Edward Albee's Plays

rather than comforting illusions. Albee also tells captivating stories via his characters' intense, passionate, nuanced monologues. Our craving for communion with others is represented by Albee's frequent use of multiple pairs of characters in his plays, while the universality of his themes and the commonality of individual human experience are highlighted by Albee's consistent use of abstracted character names, like Girl, Boy, Man, and Woman in *The Play About the Baby,* for example. Albee's work is always fresh and interesting because he makes use of alternating environments and structures through the course of his plays. He will place his characters in an open environment like a park or a beach for one play and then place them in an enclosed room for another play, but his characters are rarely able to escape the reality of their isolation regardless of their environment. Albee makes use of traditional climactic and episodic structures in his plays, but his structural tactic of moving toward a culminating center dominates his later work. Figure 1 (left) tracks Albee's use of thematic and dramaturgical motifs through each of his plays.

Each chapter of this book takes a close look at one (or a pair) of Albee's plays. Each chapter is prefaced with an outline of the play crafted from Albee's text (excepting the headings for *Everything in the Garden* and all but the headings for *A Delicate Balance*), features a brief exegesis of each section of the play, and closes with a discussion of the thematic and dramaturgical motifs articulated above. Quoted text is usually only given a citation if the text comes from outside the analyzed section. Albee frequently uses ellipses in his dialogue, and I have not distinguished between which ellipses in the quoted text are Albee's and which are mine. However, italics in quoted text are always the source's italics or Albee's stage directions. The book closes with a suggestion for staging the Albee canon, a final thought on Albee's work, and a list of Works Cited, which includes a key for page references to Albee's work throughout the book.

THE ZOO STORY

The Zoo Story

With the first line of his first published play, Albee initiates a unifying concern of his entire body of work: communicating honestly, specifically, and without illusion or compromise. Friendless Jerry, bursting with a desire to be understood, unleashes a barrage of fascinating details about his life and circumstances and what he's learned. Peter listens, mesmerized, but Peter is too far removed from Jerry's experience to offer him the empathy he desperately needs.

I. Let Me Tell You Some Things (*1CP* 15-27)

Jerry, approaching a stranger in a park, foregoes the generic *hello* for a more specific conversation-starter: "I've been to the zoo." Refusing to backtrack with a polite *excuse me*, Jerry insists that Peter acknowledge his effort to communicate by raising his voice on the third repetition of his assertion. The fact that Jerry's approach is shocking enough to seem absurd ("It always happens when I try to simplify things; people look up," *1CP* 28), even multiple decades after the play's initial production, highlights the importance we place on the comforting conventions of social niceties. Albee's playful interest in linguistic accuracy, evident in nearly all of his plays, is initiated in this first exchange as well when Jerry prompts Peter to qualify "north" with "northerly." Relentless in his honesty (or is it his manipulation of Peter's behavior?), Jerry opines that Peter's pipe-smoking might result in cancer and rejects Peter's polite dishonesty about minding if they talk. When Peter decides he really doesn't mind if they talk, the established connection so throws Jerry that he comments on the weather and repeats his opening assertion before he realizes he can now move forward and ask Peter more personal questions.

Jerry is quite perceptive at picking out Peter's private thoughts and picks away at "the veneer we call civilization" (*Counting the Ways, 2CP* 546) by reminding Peter that marriage "isn't a law, for God's sake," observing that Peter looks "like an animal man," wondering whether Peter's daughters' pet birds might "carry disease," and getting Peter to laugh at the idea that Peter might rid himself of the cats he opposes by setting diseased birds free in the house and letting feline nature take its course. Jerry continues to insist upon trust and honesty, albeit defensively. Peter's reluctant revelation of his home address is followed by Jerry's "That wasn't so hard, was it?" And four lines later Jerry snaps, "Don't my dear fellow me." But when Jerry softens a little—admitting to patronizing Peter and asking a less abrasive question—the conversation falters.

So Jerry returns to the topic of his trip to the zoo but then, prompted by what he perceives as Peter's pigeonholing of him, detours to give Peter a specifically detailed account of his life and circumstances and possessions. While these longer speeches reinforce Jerry's characterization as eclectic and obsessive, they also establish his eloquence and serve as a tune-up for the mesmerizing storytelling ability he will soon exhibit. They also give us insight into Jerry's difficult childhood, making Jerry the first of many damaged children in Albee's *oeuvre*. Since they met, Jerry has challenged Peter to examine his perceptions, to foment awareness and cull illusions and risk contact, but Jerry is not blind to his own human potential for dulling the edges of experience. Jerry says of his harrowing account, "I have no feeling about any of it that I care to admit to myself."

Peter's curiosity about Jerry's empty picture frames, symbolic of Jerry's being a "*permanent transient*" (*1CP* 32), prompts the biographical account. Albee stresses the importance of depth over surface by having Jerry complete these personal revelations before he thinks to ask Peter his name, to make the polite introductions that would normally occur at the beginning of a play. In many of his subsequent plays, Albee will abandon specific character names altogether and use generalized, abstracted names instead, like Father and Nurse in his next play, for example.

Jerry makes wry observations about our tendencies toward illusion and denial. He asserts that "when you're a kid you use the [pornographic playing] cards as a substitute for a real experience, and when you're older you use real experience as a substitute for the fantasy." After describing how his landlady "believes and relives [Jerry's suggestion of] what never happened," Peter says, "I find it hard to believe that people such as that really are," to which Jerry retorts, "It's for reading about, isn't it?" "And fact is better left to fiction." Jerry insists that Peter acknowledge his willing participation in their exchange. To Peter's "I'd rather not talk about these things" Jerry says, "So? Don't." And before Jerry launches into the dog story, he warns Peter, "You don't *have* to listen. Nobody is holding you here; remember that."

II. The Story of Jerry and the Dog (*1CP* 27-31)

Jerry makes frequent reference to the zoo to engage and keep Peter's interest (15, 17, 21, 25), but why Jerry went to the zoo (25) and what he's been meaning to tell Peter about "is the dog" (26). And to ensure Peter stays engaged through the long story, Jerry again says that "after I tell you about the dog…then I'll tell you about what happened at the zoo" (26). Jerry begins by saying that he thinks "THE STORY OF JERRY AND THE DOG…has something to do with how sometimes it's necessary to go a long distance out of the way in order to come back a short distance correctly," an assertion Jerry made earlier in reference to his physical path to the zoo (21). It was then necessary for Jerry to go out of his way to tell Peter of his life, his living conditions, and his landlady in order to come back to what he was about to say earlier: why he went (his psychological path) to the zoo.

Albee's body of work features many superb monologues, of which Jerry's is perhaps the finest, both in terms of its narrative power and its emotional intensity. Jerry relates his attempts to "overcome" the dog's "antipathy" toward him with bribes of hamburger meat. When this fails, Jerry makes an extreme tactical shift and attempts to kill the dog with poison, but then hopes that the dog will live so that he can "see what our new relationship might come to." Upon the dog's recovery, "we looked into each other's face, we made contact," Jerry loving the dog now and wanting the dog to love him, hoping "that the dog would understand," because "if you can't deal with people, you have to make a start somewhere." Then, in one of the most passionately vulnerable pleas/confessions that any of Albee's characters will make, Jerry admits how hard it is to start with "a mirror" and documents the ways in which he has struggled to make a start "in this humiliating excuse for a jail." And then, in a brilliant and crushing linguistic choice, Albee has Jerry (speaking of himself and the dog) use the same root word that characterized his hope to now characterize their loss, their compromise, their bargain, their failed contact: "[W]e have an understanding." Albee has Jerry (in summarizing his new relationship with the dog) articulate conditions in the human zoo that underlie most of the problems Albee will dramatize in his subsequent plays: "We regard each other with a mixture of sadness and suspicion, and then we feign indifference." "We neither love nor hurt because we do not try to reach each other." "If we can so misunderstand, well then, why have we invented the word love in the first place?"

III. Why I Went to the Zoo (*1CP* 31-40)

Naturally, Jerry is extremely upset when Peter says, "I DON'T UNDERSTAND!" But part of Jerry's problem is that he is possessive ("*Her* dog! I thought it was my...No. No, you're right. It *is* her dog") and defensive ("of course you don't understand") in his attempts to reach others. Jerry, who has just sat down on the bench next to Peter for the first time, intensifies their relationship by making it physical, by tickling Peter to get him to stay. Then Jerry tells Peter why he went to the zoo: "to find out more about the way people exist with animals, and the way animals exist with each other, and with people too. It probably wasn't a fair test, what with everyone separated by bars from everyone else." Jerry becomes more aggressively physical, punching Peter in the arm, to get Peter to tap into his pure, violent animal nature, goading Peter into claiming the public bench as his own.

In the heat of this conflict, Jerry continues to demand that Peter make honest assessments of his situation. When Peter asserts, "I've put up with you all afternoon," Jerry corrects, "Not really." Peter is able to self-assess that he feels ridiculous screaming for the police. Even in an open park without bars, Peter is as isolated and as trapped as an animal in a zoo. And so is Jerry. Only a mutual understanding of each other will free them. Jerry castigates Peter for making his reality about "iron and wood": "Is this the thing in the world you'd fight for? Can you think of anything more absurd?…Don't you have any idea, not even the slightest, what other people *need*?" Albee's characterization of our Absurd situation is that we crave contact even though that contact will not yield a validation or even an understanding of our identity by the others with whom we crave contact. Realizing this, Jerry initiates one last extreme tactic for making contact: to bully Peter into picking up a knife upon which Jerry, hopeless for any other meaningful contact, then impales himself, thanking Peter for comforting him. In the original script, Jerry had much more to say to Peter, but Albee wisely excised most of Jerry's dying speech and some earlier lines that implied Jerry entered the park with the intention of dying (cf. *AD/ZS* 48, 19-20). The revised text makes the events of the play less of a foregone conclusion. Jerry is able to hope for understanding until the moment he impales himself, and the shortened text emphasizes what drives Jerry through the play: his need for comfort. Jerry reciprocates Peter's comfort by urging Peter to remove evidence of his participation in Jerry's impending death and by praising him: "You're an animal, too."

Esslin says *The Zoo Story* is "marred by its melodramatic climax" and its "sentimentality, especially as [Jerry] expires in touching solicitude and fellow-feeling for his involuntary murderer" (Esslin 312). But the point of the play is that Jerry is desperate to bond with Peter. Jerry ends his story of the dog with "We neither love nor hurt because we do not try to reach each other" (*1CP* 31), and Jerry tells that story in the hope that Peter will understand that Jerry is reaching out to him.

Jerry is only defensive and abrasive with Peter because Jerry refuses to compromise his expression of stark reality, insisting that Peter see past the veneer we call civilization and identify as Jerry does with his raw animal nature. Jerry says, "[I]f you can't deal with people, you have to make a start somewhere," before cataloguing the personal objects and concepts with which he tries to identify himself in order to bond "someday, with people." His struggle with identity is highlighted by the fact that he says of one object: "a mirror…no, that's too hard, that's one of the last steps" (30). Albee's insistence upon our awareness of the reality of damaged children and his equation of reality with loss begin with Jerry, who recounts the harrowing experiences of his youth (23) and who says of his attempt at contact with the dog: "[W]hat is gained is loss" (31).

Several of Albee's recurring dramaturgical motifs are initiated in his first play: the meta-awareness that insists upon judging the accuracy or aesthetics of language even as one is using it, the riveting monologue of mesmerizing detail or emotional release or both, the feeling of being trapped or isolated even in an open environment, and the structural use of a culminating central idea in conjunction with traditional linear structures whether climactic (as here) or episodic. "Why I went to the zoo" informs every section of *The Zoo Story*: it provokes Jerry's interaction with Peter; it is the necessary response to Jerry's experience with the dog; and it asserts that facing reality requires an awareness of our animal nature.

THE DEATH OF BESSIE SMITH

The Death of
Bessie Smith

The call to face reality is a call to consciousness and action, an appeal to reach one's potential in opposition to what Albee calls closing down. But the call to face reality can be misused by those with a vested interest in dampening the potential of others. Facing reality is not simply adhering to the conditions of a racist system but rather acknowledging, resisting, and fighting the unjust power dynamic of that system. Albee's second play is about potential stalled, denied, or unrealized. Hopes articulated in the early scenes are met with resistance and then dashed or abandoned in the latter half of the play. The Nurse and the Intern are aware of their own unachieved potential and of the potential for improvements in a racist society, but their self-concern keeps them closed down and unwilling to take meaningful action.

I. On Our Way (*1CP* 45-59)

In the opening scene Jack is hopeful but tentative. His sequence of responses to Bernie's queries moves from "travelin'" to "North" to "New York" to "I got somethin' goin' up there" to "you'd be surprised." Jack has tied his hopes to Bessie making new recordings in New York and presumably delays dropping Bessie's name because he half expects Bernie's "what's she been doin' the past four-five years?" Albee keeps his high-status characters, Bessie and the mayor, offstage but also makes the power differential between black and white clear. Bessie is required to get up from her offstage bed if she wants to "go back on top again," but in the case of the mayor, bound to his hospital bed by hemorrhoids, "the seat of government is now in Room 206."

Even though the Nurse relentlessly confronts her Father with the illusion of his societal status, he still has the authority to forbid her to use his car and confronts her with her own illusions regarding the Intern's intentions. The hopeful Orderly says, "I'm going beyond that" and "there are some people who believe in action." The Nurse, embittered by her powerlessness and proclaiming that promises are lies spoken with no intention of action, invokes both existing racist tropes (referring to the Intern as "the great white doctor" and "my very own white knight") and visions of future black empowerment to break the Orderly's spirit, accusing him of betraying his heritage, calling him "an inhabitant of no-man's-land," suggesting that he has no worth outside New York "where nobody's any better than anybody else," and ordering him to get her cigarettes.

II. *Stranded...Here* (*1CP* 59-81)

The offstage crash that leads to Bessie's death occurs during a phone conversation between nurses at the two hospitals Jack will later enter, contrasting their hopeless boredom, apathy, and pettiness with the visceral loss of hope Jack experiences. The Nurse spurns the Intern's advances and his offers of marriage, the "great promise with its great conditional attached to it," suggesting that the Orderly "is in a far better position…realistically, economically…to ask to marry me than you are." Running with the idea, the Intern then uses the same racist epithet as the Nurse does to refer to the Orderly while in the same speech passing judgment on what he predicts would be her father's racist reaction and on his prediction that her father would "adjust his values" given the economic "advantages of the match." Selfishly, although the Nurse and the Intern are aware that a progressive society moves away from racist practices, they enjoy the power a racist status quo allows them to wield. Earlier the Nurse mocked the Orderly's wish to talk to the Mayor, but here she suggests that it could be advantageous to the Intern's career to do so. But the Intern, who laments that he is "*stranded…here*," has dreams of assisting the war in Spain, dreams that the Nurse dissipates. He in turn confronts her by dashing (if his assumptions are correct) the illusion of her chastity. And although the Intern discounted the Nurse's father earlier, when in her wrath the Nurse threatens to have her father take action against the Intern, he acquiesces. The Nurse uses imagery of a lynching as a metaphor for her power over the Intern, whose behavior she will now compel to support her illusions of courtship and gallantry. Of their new working relationship she says, "it'll be as though nothing had happened."

Jack first takes Bessie to the ironically named Mercy Hospital, where Second Nurse, an angel of apathy and inertia, doesn't announce that Mercy is for whites only and order Jack to leave but perhaps more insidiously simply tells him to "sit down and wait a while" as if someone might eventually see him. As Second Nurse hurls a racial slur at Jack, Nurse is doing the same to the Orderly. As the Intern upon his exit shares with the Nurse his fantasy of her coming to him with a bleeding arm that he would willfully "just hold on to…and watch your blood flow," Jack is relegated to actually, helplessly doing the same with Bessie. The Nurse taunts the Orderly and laments "a great…*abandonment*," but then she is triggered (like Jerry is triggered after taunting Peter) by the Orderly's "I don't understand you" and "you go much too far" to a moment of self-awareness: "I am sick of the disparity between things as they are, and as they should be!…I am tired of the truth…and I am tired of lying about the truth." At this point Jack arrives, and the Nurse reverts to her domineering nature except for a couple of moments when Jack's narrative about Bessie inspires her to reflect on the Intern's hurtful fantasy of her blood like "water from a faucet" (78, cf. 72) and on the music she enjoys (cf. 47-8): "I know who she is…I heard her sing."

Upon returning, the Intern defies the Nurse's warning and goes outside to check on Bessie, tersely commanding the Orderly to accompany him. The Nurse is more concerned with Jack's presence in a white hospital than with his emergency, and the absurdity of that selfishness is highlighted by Jack's simple acknowledgement: "I know, lady…you told me." The Intern's selfish concern is not with Bessie's ineligibility for admittance to the hospital but, upon discovering that she is dead, with his own lost opportunity: "WHAT WAS *I* SUPPOSED TO DO?" The Nurse resumes threatening the Intern, but he does not slap her because of the threats but rather because he cannot face the reality of her "*tuneless, almost keening*" despair. After Jack eases outside, the Orderly wonders what Jack was thinking "bringing a dead woman here." But clearly Jack was acting on the irrationality of hopelessness, something the Nurse, the Intern, and the Orderly are all experiencing: closed down, backed up, their dreams deferred.

扙 • 扙

Esslin passes over *The Death of Bessie Smith*, which he characterizes as "grimly realistic social criticism" (Esslin 312), but the absurdity of man's inability to face reality and to reach his fellow man is palpable in this play. The Nurse desires the Intern but knows that he can't offer her either gallantry or financial security. Her experiences are so far from her idea of herself that she wants out of her skin (*1CP* 74). The Intern desires medical glory but imagines it as only happening far away. He will settle for proposing to the Nurse in order to gain sexual access to her, even though he fantasizes about letting her die and slaps her for being vulnerable. The Orderly wants to take action, but if the Nurse is to be believed his actual behavior compromises his identity (57-9). Jack loses not only Bessie but his dream of a better life in New York, although the reality of that dream may have been questionable given Bessie's years of inactivity. Bessie's absence from the play signifies that the play is not about her but rather about the crisis of identity and sense of loss that this story of her death prompts in Albee's characters, and even though new facts about Bessie's death have come to light since this early work was written, the racial division characterized by Albee's play, while perhaps not as overtly articulated, still exists.

While the Nurse calls attention to the Orderly's use of the word "condone" (55), her intention is more to disrespect the Orderly than to appreciate his word choice. Jack's monologue does not exhibit the powerful storytelling or emotional release that Albee's monologues generally do, but the monologue is essential for establishing Jack's depth of character. This play initiates Albee's technique, used in about half his plays, of abstracting character names (names here preceded by an article in the character listing but not in the speech headings). The Orderly's struggle with identity is underlined by his being the only black character with an abstracted name. Albee also has Jack say again in Scene 8 a significant portion of text from Scene 7, a repetition technique he will use again later to intensify *Marriage Play* and *The Play About the Baby*. While the admissions room of the hospital requires walls, there are four other locations behind that room, of which Albee says, "*All of this very open, for the whole back wall of the stage is full of the sky*" (44). Although the play is divided into eight scenes, it occurs in a single day and progresses toward a climactic event: the revelation of Bessie's death. Because Albee wanted to keep Bessie offstage, for two brief moments he moves the driving action of the play offstage, an awkward choice he makes again only in *Fam and Yam* and (less awkwardly) at the beginning of *The Play About the Baby*. Although they are sometimes linked to their date of composition, Albee's plays are not set in specific time periods, with the exception of this one, which occurs on September 26, 1937, a Sunday.

THE SANDBOX

The Sandbox

Rituals both celebrate human experience and provide a means of coping with our fears, our losses, and our mortality. But rituals can serve both our expression and our denial of reality. There is a sense of revealing or containing the mysterious in ritual that helps us believe that we can control the uncontrollable, that everything is settled. And the repetitive nature of ritual can lead to a familiarity that dampens its power. Regardless of Mommy's efforts to cloak Grandma's impending death in comforting ritual conventions, the power and significance of the event threaten to overwhelm her: she struggles to face the reality that Grandma's time has come.

I. It's Settled (*1CP* 87-91)

The Sandbox and *The American Dream* (which also features Mommy, Daddy, Grandma, and the Young Man) call attention to the way we wield language, often violently, to settle disputes, to dictate or to deny stark reality. To Daddy's "It's cold," Mommy retorts, "Don't be silly; it's as warm as toast." To her "What do you think, Daddy?" he yields, "Whatever you say, Mommy." Mommy is determined to control the event of her mother's passing. She chooses the perfect location, orders the Musician onstage, and dictates when the Musician will or will not play. Mommy deems the sandbox the appropriate place for Grandma's placement but has no concern for Grandma's physical or mental comfort. Mommy refuses to acknowledge Grandma's distress and insists that she, Daddy, and Grandma just sit and wait. (Second Nurse distances herself from Jack's distress by ordering him to sit and wait in *The Death of Bessie Smith*.)

Grandma then speaks directly to the audience, the first of many Albee characters to do so. She challenges Mommy's dominance by asking the Musician to stop and by presenting exposition about the family situation from her point of view. In addition to acknowledging the audience, Grandma prompts the stage manager to dim the lights, keeping the audience aware that this event is staged.

II. The Time Has Come (*1CP* 91-94)

Mommy's meta-awareness of "an off-stage rumble" and her use of clichés in response to Grandma's impending death suggest that her language is more staged than sincere. But even though she speaks hollow language and summarizes the experience with "It pays to do things well," when the reality of the off-stage rumble first strikes, Mommy weeps and experiences true loss. Albee transitions quickly from Mommy's brief moment of vulnerability to humor with a blackout followed by the image of Grandma shoveling sand on herself "with this goddamn toy shovel." The fact that the ritual can be hollow and humorous in no way diminishes its power. The fact that the Young Man is an actor who acknowledges that he has (and stumbles over) "a line here" in no way diminishes his power as an Angel of Death. Powerful forces work through and in spite of humble and imperfect agents.

Two-thirds of Albee's plays will deal with marriage or family conflicts. Here, Mommy has subdued Daddy and ignores Grandma. The conflict between mother and daughter will be more palpable in *The American Dream,* as will the Young Man's concern with his identity and purpose. Here, the Young Man is not concerned with his identity—the studio hasn't given him a name yet—although he does his best to play the role he is assigned. Grandma enters in fear, but becomes calm when talking to the audience and the Young Man. Despite Mommy's attempts to cover her emotions through commands and orders and reassuring language, there is a moment when she faces the reality of her mother's impending death.

The ability of language choices to shape reality is present here—"Of course, whatever I say"—as well as the acknowledgement of the use of theatrical conventions. This play calls attention to itself as a staged ritual, which calls attention to the fact that our funeral services and other rituals are staged, that we are capable of going through their repetitive motions or experiencing them palpably or both: it's a matter of awareness and choice. Albee has his characters speak to their audiences in about half of his plays, a technique that increases both the intimacy and the scope of his work. *The Sandbox* is the first play in which all the character names are abstracted, a situation that occurs in about one-third of Albee's plays. More than one-third of Albee's plays end in death, including the first three. The first three plays are set in an open environment, and in all three "the background is the sky" (*1CP*

86). *The Sandbox* is one of only five plays in which Albee specifically calls for music (the others being *The Death of Bessie Smith*, *Who's Afraid of Virginia Woolf?*, *The Ballad of the Sad Café*, and *Malcolm*) and is the only play of the first four not to be set specifically on a Sunday.

FAM AND YAM

Fam and Yam

The Young American Playwright sharpens the weapon of his linguistic exchange with the Famous American Playwright by redefining its context: Yam asks for advice but thanks Fam for the interview. The significance of the switch is underlined by moving from the indefinite to the definite, from an article to the interview.

I. An *Indefinite* Article (*FAY* 82-90)

Yam begins by admiring Fam's paintings, his apartment, his view, his status, and the frequency of his output and by calling him a pro. Yam then attempts to bond with Fam by disparaging the general claim of an academic that "*pro* is synonymous with high-class hack" and asserting, as if the academic rather than Yam had referred to Fam as a pro, that "you and a man like that just don't talk the same language." This sets up Yam's request for advice from Fam for "an article on the theatre." Fam awkwardly attempts to reciprocate Yam's accolades.

II. The Interview (*FAY* 90-96)

Yam outlines his "attack" and his intention to "make a list of villains" to initiate the article. The mystery of the play concerns the nature of Yam's intentions. What appears to be Yam's bonding with an idol about the fact that "[e]verybody's culpable" for the theatre's problems (and Fam does indeed laugh with delight at Yam's bold assertions) might actually be Yam enlisting a playwright of status for his own ends. Once Fam validates Yam by saying he likes Yam's idea, Yam becomes serious, exits quickly, and calls back to thank Fam, not for his advice but for "the interview." Seconds later, Fam realizes the consequences of the linguistic shift: that Yam's readers will believe Fam fully agrees with Yam's opinions. The intensity of Fam's reaction is underscored by frowning, peeling, tilting, and falling artwork.

Did Yam plan this bait and switch, or is he just enthusiastic, self-absorbed, and in need of validation of his identity as a playwright? It does seem odd that a wordsmith would elide "advice" and "interview" into mutually supportive nouns. But Albee, who cut Jerry's original revelation that he may have planned his exchange with Peter, gives no definitive proof of Yam's intentions here. *Fam and Yam*, like *The Zoo Story*, features a young man challenging an older man and making him complicit in the younger man's controversial agenda.

Albee doesn't include *Fam and Yam* in his final volumes of collected plays, but the play is widely published and worthy of consideration here. Rakesh Solomon also found the play valuable, learning a great deal about Albee's directorial process from a 1978 production (Solomon 80-9), including Albee's choice to move offstage action onstage (81). While neither Yam nor Fam comment on specific word choices as they make them, the climax of the play is dependent on a revised word choice. While Yam and Fam do not prompt the stage manager as in *The Sandbox*, they each make reference to specific playwrights. This, along with Yam's castigation of everyone, constitutes an awareness of theatrical art. *Fam and Yam* is Albee's first play to occur in a confined environment and the first of only three to make direct reference to Albee the playwright or his work, the others being *Lolita* and *Fragments* (and there's an indirect reference to *Tiny Alice* in *The Goat, 3CP* 563). Albee often labels his plays; he labels this one "An Imaginary Interview." Does this mean that although Yam characterizes the exchange as an interview, it actually isn't? Or is Albee, after associating himself with Yam in the text, fending off potential speculation that an event like this actually occurred?

THE AMERICAN DREAM

The American Dream

One of Esslin's characterizations of the Theatre of the Absurd is the restoration of language to "the expression of authentic content, rather than its concealment" (Esslin 408-9). In *The American Dream*, the most Absurd of his early plays, Albee puts surface politeness into relief by exposing the blunt, selfish subtext and jostling for power underneath his characters' words. He shows how vivid, violent metaphorical imagery becomes bloodless, meaningless, and distant through repetition and then gives those images meaning and presence again through the Young Man. We can use language to express our dreams *and* to deform and corrupt them. We use language to connect with each other but also to distance ourselves from one another and, at worst, even to harm: to affect a loss of innocence, of feeling, of humanity; to close down human potential; to drain dreams of their depth.

I. The Age of Deformity (*1CP* 99-132)

The opening lines of the play establish the quintessential American couple mired in complaint about their circumstances. Mommy, like Jerry, repeats an assertion to force attention. She establishes her dominance over Daddy by demanding he listen to her story, which reveals how the chairman of her woman's club dominates her. Mommy's identification of her hat is redirected by Mrs. Barker's language game. Such is the overlap of color ranges that one can refer to a particular color as being either beige or wheat: to demand acknowledgement of one or the other is an assertion of power, a petty assertion given its triviality. Mommy's petty satisfaction comes not from attaining a new hat, but from manipulating the salespeople in the hat shop to pretend they've sold her a new one, even though it "looked exactly like" the old one. Mommy's ambivalence to reality is exemplified by her assertion that she is "terribly fond" of the "dreadful" chairman of her woman's club and by her assertion that her first hat is beige then wheat and her second hat, which she confirms is actually the first hat, is wheat then beige.

Grandma enters with nicely wrapped boxes. She suggests that dignity is essential to civilization and that disrespectful language can kill: "That's why old people die, eventually. People talk to them that way." Daddy asserts that there is a difference between what one means and what one says. Mommy relates a memory of how the false perception of her classmates—that her nicely wrapped lunch box was empty—was used to her advantage. Grandma's itemization of the contents of her boxes (143) is more poetic than literal. Albee uses the blunt expression of what is usually subtext to humorous effect. Mommy says to Daddy, "I can live off you, because I married you," and Grandma says to Mommy, "You wanted me around so you could sleep in my room when Daddy got fresh." Daddy's not wanting "to get fresh anymore" is more subservience to Mommy than impotence, though.

Mommy manipulates Daddy's hesitation to open the door—and receive "some people" for whom they have been waiting since the opening of the play—with false exhortations of his masculinity. Mrs. Barker, listening outside since the opening of the play, refers to herself in the plural, as do Mommy and Daddy. Grandma's refusal to play this game establishes her credibility. Albee has his characters use familiar polite syntax but alters their phrasing to call attention to false politeness. Mrs. Barker exclaims, "My, what an unattractive apartment you have!" When Mrs. Barker, who reminds Mommy that she is the chairman of Mommy's woman's club, shuts down Mommy's claim that Mrs. Barker's hat is not a cream hat with an assertion of power, Mommy politely invites her to disrobe ("Won't you take off your dress?), which she does ("I don't mind if I do"), prompting Daddy's "I just blushed and giggled and went sticky wet." Mommy therefore flaunts her virile but tamed husband to Mrs. Barker, whose husband does not have the use of his legs. Upon Mrs. Barker's offering to smoke, Mommy's false-polite "Oh, that isn't necessary" is countered by Mrs. Barker's false-polite "I don't mind if I do."

Albee wittily has Grandma deliver an anti-conformity epigram by replacing the expected use of the word "conformity" with a rhymed substitute: "Middle-aged people think they're special because they're like everybody else. We live in the age of deformity." (Grandma also recounts Mommy's reference to the baby that will later be dismembered as a "bumble" of joy.) This sentiment aligns with the Absurdist opposition to Esslin's half-conscious and Albee's closed-down lives. Mommy's willful denial of reality is also in opposition to Absurdist ideals. After disparaging Mrs. Barker's husband (presumably speaking without thinking), Mommy makes a show of false remorse and then says, "I won't think about it, and that way I'll forget that I ever said it, and that way it will be all right."

Albee's masterful use of language and narrative structure in Grandma's story to Mrs. Barker about a family "very much like" her own and Mrs. Barker's interjections serve as a necessary prologue and counterpoint to the uncomfortable truths the Young Man will subsequently reveal to Grandma. Grandma's story of the dismembered baby prompts a humorous recognition that our clichés, taken literally, are quite visceral and unsettling: "[I]t didn't have a head on its shoulders, it had no guts, it was spineless, its feet were made of clay…just dreadful things." The codification (desensitization through repetition) of these violent images into abstract language (clichés) distances us from their power, just as Grandma's phrase "very much like" distances Mommy and Daddy from culpability for their actions. When Mrs. Barker counters with "it isn't very much *like*…it *is*," we simultaneously laugh at Mrs. Barker's literal interpretation of the figurative language Grandma used to blur culpability in her story but also realize that we, who at our worst are very much like Mommy and Daddy, wield potentially harmful linguistic power.

II. The American Dream (*1CP* 132-148)

While the dismembered child seems a figurative device, the associated losses felt by the Young Man, the dismembered child's twin, are literal and poignant. The Young Man, a metaphor for the American Dream, is irresistibly appealing but will "do almost anything for money" and has suffered a "fall from grace…a departure of innocence." As a result of the spiritual losses he has experienced, losses which correspond to the physical losses of his twin, he is "incomplete," "can feel nothing," and is only "what you see." Moved by the Young Man, Grandma now refers to his twin as "someone very much like you," using the phrase compassionately rather than ironically. Although hollow, the Young Man is not in denial of reality. There is no false politeness in his speech, and his warning to Grandma—"What I have told you may not be true"—speaks to his self-awareness and to his function in the play as a representation of the power of metaphorical language, real and consequential even if not literally true.

The last section of *The American Dream* has some similarities to its predecessor, *The Sandbox*. The action is set in motion by Mrs. Barker's "the whole thing's settled" (cf. 87); the lights dim to mark the significance of Grandma's departure, and Mommy has a brief moment of honest vulnerability (cf. 92); and Grandma speaks to the audience. Several motifs recur to close the play. Daddy keeps his distance from the Young Man to signify his sexual repression. Mommy and Mrs. Barker have one last exchange of false politeness. Mommy says the Young Man is "much better than the other one" (although she "can't quite place" why he looks familiar), indicating that he is simply a measure of her satisfaction, no more significant than her hat. Mommy implies that the Young Man might serve as an instrument of her satisfaction as well, this impending incest another metaphor for how the pursuit of a hollow American dream can end in moral vacancy. Grandma closes the play with an observation that could serve as a comment on the denial of reality inherent in living the American dream: "[E]verybody's got what he thinks he wants."

Esslin characterizes *The American Dream* as an attack that "pours scorn on the sentimental ideals of family life" and characterizes the Young Man as "a replacement for the adopted child that went wrong and died" (Esslin 312). The play is actually about the absurdity of longing for human contact but only being able to act on that longing, to reach out or to listen, when one is near death or so drained of feeling that the risks of rejection inherent in attempted contact are nullified. The tender exchanges between Grandma and the Young Man in both *The Sandbox* and *The American Dream* are rare expressions of two people being able to reach an understanding in Albee's plays. Our propensity to betray each other keeps us from reaching each other: the adopted child didn't go wrong; he was done wrong.

Albee treats wife-husband conflict and mother-child conflict farcically here, but realistic versions of these family conflicts become a signature motif in most of his subsequent plays. Mommy, Daddy, and Mrs. Barker bury the reality of their losses and fears in trivialities and false-politeness, while the Young Man accurately describes but cannot feel the severity of his losses. The Young Man is so thoroughly damaged that he has no identity: he "cannot relate" but "must be related *to*"; he is "incomplete" and only "what you see."

While the characters in this play do not comment on their linguistic choices, Albee uses their linguistic power games, false politeness, and self-absorbed expression of subtext to make us aware of the way we use language as a weapon and as a means of denying reality. He contrasts this misuse of language with Grandma's truthful reflections and wisdom—especially when she speaks to the Young Man or to the audience—and with the Young Man's wrenching articulation of his losses in another riveting Albee monologue. The setting for this play, while perhaps sparser than most of Albee's living rooms, is still confining: Daddy doesn't "even want to sleep in the apartment" (108) that Grandma finds it necessary to escape.

WHO'S AFRAID OF
VIRGINIA WOOLF?

III. The Exorcism

Who's Afraid of Virginia Woolf?

Ge*orge and Martha's identities are wrapped up in the games they play with each other and with other people. But these games become dark rituals because the ongoing, predictable story of humanity involves a fight against the "corruption of weakness and petty revenges" in which "Weakness, imperfection cries out against strength, goodness and innocence" (*1CP* 301, 299). And when our illusions are exorcised and our games are ended, there may not be much of an identity to work with because we've been so dependent on our games.

I. Fun and Games (*1CP* 155-212)

The play opens with the game of Martha quizzing George about a film she can't identify. George laments his required ritual attendance at "these goddamn Saturday night orgies" of Martha's father, parties at which the substitution of "Virginia Woolf" for "big bad wolf" in a children's rhyme are considered witty, at least by Martha. Martha laments George's refusal to play the political games that are the *raison d'etre* of her father's parties. All of Martha and George's interactions are games, usually verbal—"walking what's left of our wits" (175)—although the threat of physical violence exists, too (consider also the toy gun, 192). Although Martha disparages George throughout the play, she admits that she "fell for him" (209) and is hurt by his dismissal of her invitation to intimacy as simply "blue games for the guests" (193). George (like Grandma, cf. 119) believes that everyone being the same is a deformity, and he grills his post-party guest, biologist Nick, about the game of "making everyone the same," "rearranging my genes, so that everyone will be like everyone else" (177-8), asserting that everyone will tend to look like Nick and that history will lose "its glorious variety and unpredictability" (198-9). This play is essentially about humanity's inevitable tendency to weakness or decline, reflected in George's assertion to Martha about the evolutionary ladder: "you can't reverse yourself...start back up once you're descending" (187).

II. Walpurgisnacht (*1CP* 213-272)

The stories we tell, our rituals, our games, can be used to reveal our identities or to deny reality. George's story about the bergin-drinking boy who accidentally kills his parents and now lives in an asylum (216-218) is revealed by Martha to be from a "book about a boy who murders his mother and kills his father, and pretends it's all an accident," a book that documents "the truth," something that "really happened" to George (246-7; cf. "You used to drink bergin, too," 236). Later, when George references his parents, Nick's challenge of "Was this before or after you killed them?" is met with George's "Maybe" (284). The use of personal stories to cultivate ambiguities of identity and reality will recur in *The Play About the Baby*. Albee is also concerned with ambiguities of identity and reality in *Tiny Alice*, and seeds of ideas for that play can be found here. Nick says that his father-in-law, a preacher, "spent God's money…and he saved his own." George says that Martha's father's second wife "was a very old lady with warts who was very rich" and "married the white mouse" (226-7; cf. George's reference to Martha's immortal father, 180). When Nick says Martha never mentioned a stepmother, George counters, "Well…maybe it isn't true" (227).

Things become more primal as the night moves on. George characterizes Nick and Martha's "familiar dance" as "a very old ritual." As George angrily resists Martha's revelations about his story, Honey calls for "Violence! Violence!" four times and is disappointed when George and Martha's physical struggle is broken off by Nick (242-7). George retaliates with "a little game of Get the Guests" in which he, under the pretense of describing his "second novel," betrays Nick's confidential relation of Honey's "hysterical pregnancy" (216) and asserts that Honey actually had an abortion, citing this failed potential as an example of the "patterns of history" (249-254; cf. "do you believe that people learn nothing from history," 178).

In Albee's plays, brief moments of self-awareness and potential connection with others are doomed to be undercut by our protective, isolationist tendencies. George challenges Nick to confront himself ("*you* almost think you're serious, and it scares the hell out of you"), tries to "reach" him, to "make contact" (consider Jerry's "We neither love nor hurt because we do not try to reach each other"), and is insulted in return. George sees their exchange as a metaphor for the limits of civilization (230-2). Later, George counters Nick's challenge of "I'll be what you say I am" with "You are already…you just don't know it." When George rejects Martha's assertion that he married her so that she could humiliate him, she counters, "DON'T YOU KNOW IT, EVEN YET?" George accuses Martha of moving "bag and baggage into your own fantasy world." Martha says to George, "There was a second back there…when I could have gotten through to you, when maybe we could have cut through all this crap. But that's past, and now I'm not going to try.…[T]here is no moment any more when we could…come together" (256-61). The threats at the end of the act are accompanied by George's citation of a passage about the fall of the West.

III. The Exorcism (*1CP 273-311*)

The motif of potential being undercut by isolationism or self-focus is also evident in the last act of the play. Martha tells Nick that he is "no better than anybody else" and says that he is just another in a long line of men with potential who, when faced with the career-enhancing prospect of a liaison with Martha, cannot perform. Nick prefers the isolation of a microscope to the communication of a microphone (cf. Nick's correction of Martha's malapropism, 277), seeing "everything but the goddamn mind." Martha cries "deep inside, so no one can see me," and although she admits that George is the only man who can make her happy, she relates several vivid examples of her absolute opposition to him because he has made "the insulting mistake of loving me and must be punished for it." When Martha lashes out at Nick, he calls it "Aimless . . . butchery." George's "Vicious children, with their oh-so-sad games" suggests that our impulses to argue and attack, that our failures of potential, are innate (273-81). George refers to Nick and Honey as "the tots" and has a toddler-like exchange with Honey just before initiating his last game (290-1).

Martha answers Nick's charge of craziness with "'tis the refuge we take when the unreality of the world weighs too heavy on our tiny heads" (275). George counters Martha's "Truth and illusion, George; you don't know the difference" with "No; but we must carry on as though we did" (285). George prompts Martha to tell the story of their child, an illusion that has become no different than truth for Martha, and intersperses the litany of an exorcism into her narrative. When Martha tries to stop, George picks up the thread of the story, using it to attack Martha. Martha asserts that she has raised her son against "the corruption of weakness and petty revenges," her defense reaching a crescendo as George completes the exorcism simultaneously with her speech (294-302). Finishing the game, George tells Martha that he has received a telegram relating the death of their son, to which Martha howls, "YOU CANNOT DO THAT!" Martha fights until the following exchange—

> MARTHA: HE IS OUR CHILD!
> GEORGE: AND I HAVE KILLED HIM!
> MARTHA: NO!
> GEORGE: YES!

—after which she is spent. George answers Martha's "Why?" with "You broke our rule…you mentioned him to someone else" (302-7). (Albee will extend this single exchange of "no" and "yes" into a chilling ritual in *The Play About the Baby, 3CP* 532-3.) George sends Nick and Honey home, and the last exchange between George and Martha, in a radical change of tempo, occurs "*very softly, very slowly.*" Martha doubts George's assertion that "It will be better" and closes with an admission of her fear in answer to the play's titular question.

࿐ • ࿐

In *Who's Afraid of Virginia Woolf?* George and Martha participate in base, mean-spirited games rather than acknowledge their need for each other. Martha's aggressive flirtation with Nick makes George jealous, and jealous George retaliates with vengeance instead of giving Martha the tenderness she craves, fueling Martha's further ugliness in a vicious cycle. George smugly asserts "I hate hypocrisy" (*1CP* 254) to justify his accusation that Honey's pregnancy was non-hysterical and self-terminated. But George is also a hypocrite, aware of the moral vacancy of the games he plays but playing them anyway. When George tries "to reach" Nick, boldly asserting "*you* almost think you're serious and it scares the hell out of you" (230-2), Nick rejects George's call for self-awareness and chooses to stay in his self-focused game. When Honey runs out, upset by George's accusation, self-focused Nick castigates George's actions as "DAMAGING!! TO ME!!" (255) Honey drowns her self-awareness in drink, but honesty surfaces through her lowered defenses. In tears, she says, "I want a child" (298), but there is a contradiction between her desire and doubts about what her self-focused husband can offer her and their child. George's exorcism of the illusion that he and Martha have a son is potentially a first step toward exorcising all the damaging games they play. There is hope for their relationship as they end the play in an honest moment together, but what happens at Martha's father's next party, when they'll be under public pressure to deny their mutual need? The fact that the impulse for the exorcism sprang from vengeful motives is not encouraging.

Albee's plays are unflinchingly honest about the inseparability of conflict from the bond of meaningful personal relationships, especially marriage. Nick and Honey's situation is even bleaker than George and Martha's because their resistance to marital conflict equates to a denial of reality more serious than George and Martha's pretense of having a son, although George and Martha's use of their imaginary son as a weapon against each other is certainly unhealthy. Their son is imaginary, but if he were real, his circumstances would be abusive (cf. 300-1). Honey's deception of Nick (if George is right) about a real, aborted child and repression of her animal nature (which surfaces with her excitement over potential violence; cf. other references to animal nature on 215, 221) make her less free than Martha, who is able to face the reality of her attraction/opposition to George and to admit that she is afraid upon giving up the illusion of her son. Nick's self-concern makes him less capable of facing reality than George. But Martha, unloved by her father (300), punishes George for loving her (277) and calls his identity into question because his motives aren't as shallow as younger men like Nick: "[I]f you existed, I'd divorce you....I haven't been able to see you for years" (164); "I watched you, and *you* weren't *there!*" (261)

George and Martha occasionally exhibit Albee's signature concern with linguistic choices. Consider Martha's sarcastic "PHRASE-MAKER!" (162) and justification of the use of abstruse "[i]n the sense of recondite" (196). George asks Martha to "show [Honey] where we keep the...euphemism" (172), corrects Nick's "gangle" to "gaggle" (230), and justifies his use of "got" versus "gotten" (267). There are a couple of nods to other plays: the poker night of Williams's *Streetcar* (273, cf. Gussow 161) and a reference to Ophelia's flowers with "violence" substituted for "violets" (281; cf. also Illyria, 180). Albee's exploration of the rituals and games that make up a marriage, one of the dominant concerns of his work, begins in earnest with this play, the blistering repartee of which is occasionally tempered with reflective monologues: George's rumination about his youth, laments for the unrealized potential of civilization (George) and of civilized lunk-heads (Martha), and

Martha's elegy for George. Albee intensifies the climactic exorcism with simultaneous dialogue and raised (all-cap) volume, then radically softens and slows the final sequence of the play. Albee will continue to explore marital dynamics in his plays by contrasting couples, as he does here with Nick and Honey and George and Martha, whose status as an iconic American couple Albee signifies by naming them after the first U.S. presidential couple (cf. the resonance of the names of *Marriage Play*'s Jack and Gillian with the iconic nursery rhyme couple). Although the play builds to an intense climax, it can also be said to culminate around the central themes of lost potential, ambiguous identities, and a lack of discernment between truth and illusion.

THE BALLAD OF THE SAD CAFE

The Ballad of the
Sad Cafe

Three of Albee's next five plays are adaptations of other authors. Albee is quite faithful to Carson McCullers's dark story about how desire can alter our identities and how unreciprocated desire moves us through conflict back to solitude. Albee's narrator frames the story with announcements of its beginning and end, just as Jerry did for the story of Jerry and the dog.

I. Far Off and Estranged (*1CP* 317-357)

A play must always be happening in the present moment, so Albee uses a narrator who speaks to the audience. But this story is about loneliness and distance, so the narrator must invoke those qualities in his opening speech. Albee has the narrator speak only to us and not to the other characters; all other Albee characters who speak to the audience, Grandma and those to come, speak to at least one other character in the play. The narrator describes the town as "like a place that is far off and estranged from all other places in the world." Miss Amelia looks out from the second-story window of a boarded-up house for an hour or so and likely sees no one on the street below. The narrator then begins to describe events eight years in the past.

The narrator also characterizes reality as something dark and hidden. Of the effect of Miss Amelia's liquor he says, "Things that have gone unnoticed, thoughts that have been harbored far back in the dark mind, are suddenly recognized and comprehended....A man may suffer, or he may be spent with joy—but he has warmed his soul and seen the message hidden there" (325). He also refers to a few of the townspeople "whose minds had darker corners than they dared dream of" (341).

The arrival of a dwarf who claims to be related to Miss Amelia triggers a change of personality in her. Like Martha breaking a rule by speaking of her son, "Miss Amelia broke her rule" (339) of forbidding the in-house consumption of her wares, turning her store into a café where the townspeople could eat and drink. "Miss Amelia had, for many years, before the arrival of Cousin Lymon, lived a solitary life," but now she loved Cousin Lymon—the first of three cases of unrequited love in the play—and shared all but one part of her life with him (348).

II. Who Is Marvin Macy? (*1CP* 357-387)

It turns out that many years ago, Miss Amelia inspired a thuggish mill-worker named Marvin Macy to reform his character and ask for her hand in marriage, which she offhandedly accepted; this is the second case of unrequited love in the play. The lack of awareness on the part of both characters concerning this event is underscored by the fact that they can neither name nor smell the flowers that Marvin offers as part of his proposal (367-8). Although Amelia accepts Marvin's proposal, he is only allowed to refer to her as "Miss Amelia," not "Amelia" (370). This is still the condition she places on all the townspeople save Cousin Lymon (339). (There will be a distinction between the use of "Miss Alice" and "Alice" in Albee's next play.) No tactic will bring Macy closer to Miss Amelia, and he must express his passion at a distance via a letter he dictates to his brother: "I hate you with all the power of my love for you" (384), sentiments that could also apply to other Albee couples, although perhaps not in the first ten days of their marriages.

III. Heat...and Silence (*1CP* 387-417)

The third case of unrequited love occurs when Cousin Lymon becomes enamored of Marvin Macy, especially given that Macy has returned from the penitentiary. (Macy returned to his old impulses after being spurned by Miss Amelia.) Cousin Lymon romanticizes the chain gang because "they are together, those men, an'...an' how they *sing*, Amelia," expressing his desire with an ecstasy that is clearly dismissive of the "good life together" he has with Miss Amelia (391). The narrator asserts that "love is a solitary thing" (393).

The narrator describes the rituals of Miss Amelia and Marvin Macy circling each other without coming to blows (405). Miss Amelia admits to Macy's brother Henry that she already would have driven Marvin off if not for her fear that Cousin Lymon would go with him and leave her "all alone," but that now she's got to drive Marvin off or kill him (408-9). When Merlie Ryan (who, like Honey, relishes impending violence; 401, 414) asks why Miss Amelia and Marvin Macy are going to kill each other, a townsperson says it's because "they know each other" (412). Their epic battle (which foreshadows the one in *Marriage Play*, *2CP* 282-3) is tilted in Macy's favor when Cousin Lymon jumps in and chokes Miss Amelia. Macy and Cousin Lymon ransack the café before leaving town (413-5). Miss Amelia drives away customers because she believes they only want to look "at the freak" (416; which resonates with *The Man Who Had Three Arms, 3CP* 193), and the narrator closes the play where it began.

Miss Amelia, Marvin Macy, and Cousin Lymon all completely disregard the contradiction between their desires and what the objects of their desire can offer them—the reality that there is no bond, only conflict—and find themselves in a harsh, ugly, unrequited love triangle that ends in vengeful violence. All three adapt their identities under the spell of their desire, and all three respond with primal, animal violence when their desires are unfulfilled.

The narrator's eloquent, reflective monologues balance the base, simplistic perspectives of the other characters. Albee uses characters like the narrator to speak directly to his audiences, and he sometimes uses his stage directions to give his readers a sense of choices being made in the present moment, as when Cousin Lymon turns on Miss Amelia and is "*almost savage; yes, savage*" (389). Although Miss Amelia begins and ends the play in self-confinement, the play occurs in an open environment to support its episodic nature. Still, Albee requires only a unit set, and the play's seamless narrative flow and build to violence would make it equally climactic in nature if not for the scope of events that are represented.

TINY ALICE

Tiny Alice

Albee characterizes *Tiny Alice* as "perfectly straightforward" (in response to critics who find the play "opaque") and as being about "the relationship of faith to sexual hysteria and the nonexistence of a god created by man in his own image" (*1CP* 8). This is another manifestation of the gap between our desires and what the world (or God or other people) can offer us, between personal fantasy or experienced sensation and unknowable abstraction. We imagine ourselves as free as birds and willing to sacrifice to something greater than ourselves, unwilling to accept the reality that our subjective desires are a cage that limits the nature and scope of our sacrifice and our faith. While the play is not opaque, there is a palpable uncertainty about what is real and what is not; this mystery underlies Albee's masterful orchestration of menace, ritual, and vivid imagery, capable of invoking unease and perhaps even fear in his readers.

I. Little Bird (*1CP 423-469*)

The opening scene is a battle between an agent of the divine and an agent of the material world, made personal by the fact that Cardinal and Lawyer were physically intimate when they were in school together. Lawyer believes that anyone can be bought and that everyone's faith is false, taunting Cardinal with the promise of great wealth for the church and, upon being called "Satan," with "You would believe it…if you believed in God." Lawyer wins the battle when Cardinal, reeling from the offer of "a billion a year for twenty years," stops being a representative of the church and speaks to Lawyer in the first-person singular, reserved "for intimates, equals…or superiors." While Cardinal doesn't realize that his agreement to send his secretary and old friend Brother Julian to Miss Alice is a sacrifice, he will be enlisted in the end to seal Julian's fate.

There are more menacing and mysterious exchanges in the second scene. Upon entering the library, Butler, who "*moves about with a kind of unbutlerlike ease,*" joins Julian in admiring the "sealed" model that is an exact replica of the castle in every way, featuring a one-to-one correspondence of rooms. Lawyer joins them and presses Julian to fill in the blanks of the six years missing from the report they have on him. Julian's defense of Cardinal, whom Lawyer disparages, prompts Lawyer's warning against confusing "the representative of a…thing with the thing itself" (which Julian will do when he thinks he has married Miss Alice). After Lawyer leaves, Julian confides to Butler that for those six years he put himself in a mental home, he "was out of reach, unreachable, finally unreaching" (again consider Jerry's "We neither love nor hurt because we do not try to reach each other"), and that he "could not reconcile myself to the chasm between the nature of God and the use to which men put… God," meaning "God the creator, not the God created by man." Julian concludes, "My faith and my sanity…they are one and the same."

Miss Alice presents to Julian in her sitting room as a *"withered crone"* (confer that "she has no intention of dying" and that her wedding gown is "two hundred years old"; 431, 523) before removing her wig and mask, a "little lightness to counter…weighty matters." Miss Alice reveals that Butler was a former lover and that she is presently mistress to Lawyer (confer references to the frequency of Alice's marriages: "all the little people running around inside" the model and "what a large family" Alice has; 471, 526). Julian describes himself as a servant and shares with Miss Alice his experience in the asylum of hallucinations "brought on by the departure of my faith, and this in turn was brought on by the manner in which people mock God." Julian characterizes his hallucinations, which are accompanied by a loss of sensory capacity (hearing replaced by roaring), as taking him "away from myself" but "never far enough"; and he describes an associated feeling of sadness and "Loss, great loss," which is an indicator of Julian's inability to deny his subjective self in service to his faith. Miss Alice suggests that Julian's troubled uncertainty—"I imagined so many things, or…did so many things I thought I had imagined"—is "what passes for sanity." He is uncertain of the reality of a sexual encounter in the asylum involving a woman who thought she was the Virgin Mary and who after the encounter believed herself to be "pregnant with the Son of God." In a chilling metaphor for the failure of Julian's faith, the woman was diagnosed with "cancer of the womb." And yet Julian's earnestness and longing for faith have made him the objective of a sinister game being played by Lawyer, Butler, and Miss Alice, who refers to Julian as "Little recluse" and "Little bird."

II. Sacrifice Yourself (*1CP* 470-509)

The second act begins with Lawyer in another battle for dominance, this time in a losing effort with Miss Alice. Lawyer continues his sexual aggression unfazed by Miss Alice's assertions of his self-absorption and distance: "impersonality in the most personal things," "selfish, hurtful." But when Miss Alice suggests that "your body is as impersonal as your...self—dry, uncaring, rubbery...dead," this negation of his physical potential and association with the final reality that no one wants to face stops him and forces him into a moment of reflection before Butler joins them in the library, underlining lost (sexual) potential by describing the wine cellar: "bottles have burst, are bursting, corks rotting....Some great years, popping, dribbling away, going to vinegar under our feet." After Julian enters, Butler suggests that the castle is a replica of the model housed in the castle (Miss Alice refers to the castle as a resonance of the model), and Lawyer suggests that the only limit to possibility is "your concept of reality," which prompts a taunt from Miss Alice and an outburst from Lawyer, after which he asserts, "abstractions *are* upsetting." Julian notices the chapel in the model on fire, which prompts urgent action to put out the corresponding fire in the castle while Miss Alice, alone with the model, alternates between prayer and conversation, supplicating herself to her ongoing pain— "the hurt the same, the name and the face changing" (cf. Lawyer's "Everything *hurts*," 474)—and to the unknown: "I have tried to obey what I have not understood." Julian, returning to report the fire has been put out, thrice says, "I don't understand," and asks, "Why, why did it happen that way—in both dimensions?" Miss Alice (recalling the imagery of Julian's hallucination, cf. 464) holds her arms out to Julian and asks for help. She invites Julian to stay in the castle, and although frightened, Julian accepts.

Of Lawyer's jealously of Julian, Butler chides, "[Y]ou're acting like the man you wish you were...[f]eeling things you can't feel." Of Lawyer's "She's *using* Julian! To humiliate me," Butler observes, "Humiliate;

not hurt," revealing Lawyer's feelings as more possessiveness than love (cf. Lawyer's equation of these, 471; but cf. also his hurt, 474). The plot against Julian involves converting him to the truth as espoused by Lawyer: that God is an abstraction that can neither be understood nor worshipped. To personify the abstraction is to limit and demean it. But, Lawyer intends to say, "There is Alice, Julian. That can be understood. Only the mouse in the model....Only the mouse, the toy. And that does not exist...but it is all that can be worshipped" (495). Excepting this statement, all other behavior in the play suggests that Alice, the force inside the model, is real, including Lawyer's address to the model, "You will have your Julian" (496). It is suggested that failure to accept Alice will be dangerous to Julian. Lawyer and Butler decide to enlist Cardinal in Julian's conversion, his marriage to Alice via Miss Alice. Of the revelation of Alice to Cardinal, Butler asks, "How much can he take?" Lawyer replies, "He is a man of God, however much he simplifies" (494).

In order to prime Julian for Alice, Miss Alice must move him from self-conscious eroticism and fantasies of surrender to real, total sacrifice. Miss Alice cites the "mental sex play" of her youth inspired by a Lawrence poem and laments the imitative, literary quality of the sex play of her experience. Julian is conscious of the sensual gluttony he is experiencing and wonders if he is "being temp—tested in some fashion." Miss Alice reminds him of his service to his church while simultaneously luring him into characterizing his experience as a temptation (physical) rather than as a test (mental). Julian speaks of his longing "to be of great service," and Miss Alice calls him on the literary nature of his speech. Julian speaks abstractly of his service, of wanting to leave a "memory of someone who helped." Miss Alice flirtatiously calls him a liar and cites the visceral history of church martyrs,

"death-seekers and hysterics: the bloodbath to immortality." She leads
Julian into a vivid discussion of his violent, erotic dream of sacrifice, thrice
whispering "Marry me" into his ear, unheard. When she puts her arms around
him, he comes out of his reverie and resists Miss Alice's "Alice needs you and
your sacrifice," but he eventually moves from saying "no...sacrifice" to "in...
my...sacrifice" as Miss Alice enfolds him in the *"great wings"* of her black
negligee, repeating Lawyer's promise to Alice: "He will be yours."

III. Accept It (*1CP* 510-548)

As the third act begins, Julian believes he has just married Miss
Alice. Cardinal, who officiated Julian's marriage to Alice, asks Lawyer,
referring to the model, "Then it is...really true? About...*this*?" Lawyer
responds, "Can't you accept the wonders of the world? Why not of this
one, as well as the other?...Since the wedding was [in the model] and
we are [in the castle] we have come quite a...dimension, have we not?"
Julian says that he feels lost and describes his experience to Butler as
"one moment married, flooded with white, and...then...the next, alone."
Butler, in a question perhaps resonant with Lawyer's to Cardinal, asks,
"When you're locked in the attic, Julian, in the attic closet, in the dark, do
you care who comes?" Julian speaks to Cardinal of the newfound "joy I
thought possible only through martyrdom," "not losing God's light" but
joining it with the ecstasy of a new light. But Lawyer notes that Julian is
no longer in church robes but "in city clothes...banker's clothes." Cardinal
exhorts Julian to "accept what you do not understand" and like Lawyer,
Butler, and Miss Alice, distances himself from Julian via the "ceremony
of Alice," through which Julian will join Alice's "large family." Lights go
on in the model's rooms during the ritual, in which Lawyer speaks of
a "union whose spiritual values shall be uppermost," and Julian says,
"[O]ur humility returns to us when we are faced with the mysteries."

After the ceremony, Julian is ritually pressured to accept the consequences of his marriage: the reduction of his faith in an abstract God to faith in a smaller abstract entity that can be associated with concrete perception (bound in a model with rooms lighted and warm) and the sensual enlargement of this entity (tiny Alice) via Miss Alice (whom, Butler says, Julian might use as a play god) so that Julian might understand and accept his sacrifice. This reduction of God to a wonder that can be seen and touched is exactly what Julian has fought against all his life (531), a fight perhaps at odds with Julian's fantasies of tactile martyrdom. When Julian asserts that there is nothing in the model, Lawyer battles back, "*She* is there…we believe." The fate of Alice's servants is tied to Julian's agreement to "Stay with her," a commitment that will "Allow us all to rest." Cardinal, having accepted money for the church, backs up Lawyer's insistence that Julian's acceptance is an "act of faith" by adding "in God's will," but upon Julian's vehement resistance, Cardinal shifts from the plural that represents the church to the personal, "We…(*Harder tone*) I *order* you." Julian laments, "I cannot have so misunderstood my life," and wonders whether he was more rational during his time in the asylum. Julian's declaration that he will return to the asylum prompts Lawyer to shoot him rather than allow him to leave.

Lawyer prompts Cardinal's exit with his taunt "You *will* go on, won't you," implying that all things good and bad, including Cardinal's complicity in Julian's demise, will be blacked out upon his death. As the trio prepares for the "same mysteries, the evasions, the perfect plotting" in a new location and for probable return to the castle "when the weather changes" (because Julian wouldn't stay?), Miss Alice asks, "For how long?" Lawyer replies, "Until we are replaced.…Or until everything is desert" (cf. Butler's "On…and on…we go," 490). Julian observes that consciousness is pain. Julian castigates Lawyer with "Instrument!" upon Lawyer's exit, but had celebrated his own function as an instrument earlier (517). Butler kisses Julian's forehead before leaving, and Miss Alice remains in the library but out of Julian's sight until the lights begin to go off in the model. Julian observes that he has only imagined death ("not being") in the abstract but not the concrete "act of…dying." (Albee will return to this idea, especially in *All Over.*) Before leaving, Lawyer had placed Miss Alice's wig from her first meeting with Julian on a phrenological head in the library. Julian wonders if the wigged head's stare is the true look and Miss Alice's "warm flesh…not real" (an interesting stage picture, given that phrenology used to be considered true, and then it was not). As Julian hears heartbeats and breathing, he demands the presence of either God or Alice. Lawyer had predicted Julian would "take what he gets for…what he wishes it to be," but Julian struggles to the end to understand what is happening to him, calling for both God and Alice. After the "*lights descend a stairway in the model*" and "*the shadow of a great presence [fills] the room*," Julian says, "I accept thee, Alice, for thou art come to me. God, Alice…I accept thy will." During the first run of the play, Albee said that Julian

> is left with pure abstraction—whatever it be called: God, or Alice—and in the end, according to your faith, one of two things happen: either the abstraction is proved real, or the dying man, in the last necessary effort of self-delusion creates and believes in what he knows does not exist. (Gussow 214)

But what does it mean that the heartbeats and breathing continue for three beats after Julian's death?

∞ • ∞

Tiny Alice explores the contradiction between our pure impulses to submit to something or someone outside ourselves and our self-focused distress over the uncertainty and vulnerability that accompany those impulses, and explores the contradiction between our individual abstract beliefs and a reality that is determined by concrete sensation and shaped by other people. Faith requires submission to what we cannot understand, to what we cannot control, to something or someone outside the self, but we are too self-focused and tied to a reality of concrete sensation to sustain such a submission. So we either retreat into the self or submit to what we can understand; and because we need the validation of others, we disseminate our beliefs through persuasion or force. Julian thinks he wants to serve and be forgotten, but his fantasies of martyrdom are visceral and sensory, and in the end he chooses the sensual reality before him rather than an abstract ideal: he cannot resist submission to Miss Alice. Lawyer, Butler, and Miss Alice are united in reorienting the beliefs of others to conform to their own need to worship what they can understand: "the mouse in the model," a deity in a box. This reshaping of reality requires great power, which requires great wealth and influence: "All legal, all accomplished, all satisfied, that which we believe" (532, 534). Alice seems omnipotent: the arrangement that initiates Julian's end is "one of several" (432); her disciples are bound south to the "house on the ocean, the…same mysteries, the evasions, the perfect plotting" and will probably return to the castle of Julian's demise (539, 543). All the relationships in this play (not really family relationships, but cf. 526) are strained and fraught with tension, but Julian's impending death elicits tenderness from Miss Alice and Butler, respect for the only mystery they can't control. Regardless of what we believe, Julian's reality is ours: a reality of loss, fear, and eventual death.

The play concerns our animal nature in that our inseparability from concrete sensation keeps us from the attainment of complete faith in an entity that can't be proved to affect the senses. There are references to animals in the first scene (cardinals, swine, hyena), to the mouse in the model, and to horses and lions in the seduction scene. Julian's identity and his reality (his sanity) are inextricably tied to his faith, but "the manner in which people mock God" (463) affects his faith. In the asylum, Julian was often uncertain of the truth of his experiences, whether they were hallucinations or reality. There are references to the ways we manufacture, filter, or limit reality: Butler chides Lawyer for "acting like the man you wish you were"; Lawyer says Cardinal will take "however much he simplifies"; Miss Alice laments literary presentation substituted for honesty; and Lawyer asserts that those "looking terror and betrayal straight in the eye" will "face the inevitable and call it what they have always wanted" (522).

The characters pay close attention to language in the play and often use language to serve their power plays. "Bequest" is amended to "arrangement" (432) and "grant" (447). Lawyer chides Butler, "There's no such word as screep" (446). Butler analyzes the length and content of Lawyer's metaphor (448-9). Of meta-awareness in general, Lawyer speaks of confusing "the representative of a…thing with the thing itself." He refers to Cardinal, but the metaphor also works for the model (or for the castle, cf. 480-1). There is a "model of the model" (439) in the model's library. Albee says the model is "the symbol for everything being part of something infinitely larger and smaller than itself" (Gussow 230). In addition to the linguistic battles of wit, Miss Alice plays "a little game" upon meeting Julian in which her disguise resonates with Alice's ancient nature. There are many rituals: Miss Alice's prayer, the seduction scene, the ceremony of Alice, the pressuring of Julian to accept and stay with Alice, and the ongoing routine of service to Alice. While much attention has been paid to Julian's final monologue (cf. Gussow 216-8, 231), Julian's recollections and fantasies (462-5, 506-8), although they include interjections from Miss Alice, are better exemplars of the mesmerizing quality of Albee's monologues. The abstractly-named Cardinal, Lawyer, and Butler (note the acknowledgement of Butler's abstract name when Julian first meets him) may be meant to represent the universal need for and approach to status in human relationships. However, Albee said in 1996, "I'm still troubled as to who those three people in the house are" (Gussow 230), and how those three came to be in Alice's service remains mysterious. This play is perhaps Albee's most lavish, with three locations (two of which must reflect great wealth), each physically expansive but psychologically confining. Albee acknowledges in his stage directions for Cardinal's garden that each production of the play will create its own environment: "*What is needed…?*" (423). Even with seven scenes played across more than one day, the play's singular focus makes it more climactic than episodic, and the recurring themes of how one struggles to determine what is real and what is not and of how the sensual, communal experience of reality is an obstacle to faith are the culminating centers of the play.

MALCOLM

Malcolm

In contrast to *The American Dream*'s Young Man, *Malcolm*'s protagonist, in Albee's adaptation of the James Purdy novel, retains his innocence, so resistant to corruption that the maturity forced on him by his marriage—and his inability to reconcile himself to loss, especially the loss of his father—results in his death. The other characters adore selfless Malcolm, but they also have a latent desire to corrupt Malcolm and remove reminders of their own lost innocence.

I. The Look of Innocence (*1CP* 553-607)

Malcolm sits on a golden bench in front of a hotel when he is approached by Cox. He tells Cox he is "waiting for nobody at all" and that his "father has disappeared," which suggests that Malcolm knows he'll never see his father again (so does the fact that Malcolm's father left him eighteen years of clothes: "I think he had a presentiment he'd be called away," 564). But he hopes to see his father. When Cox says "don't tell me you've been waiting for *him*," Malcolm realizes, "Yes; perhaps I may be waiting for *him*." Cox, an agent of corruption, says that innocence and stupidity "are easily confused, and people will take the easy road, Malcolm, and find you stupid. Innocence must go!" "You must… give yourself up to things." Malcolm agrees to accept the arrangements Cox makes for him to meet people.

The Raphaelsons, Kermit and Laureen, are the first of three eccentric couples to whom Cox sends Malcolm. The Raphaelsons, who were happy before they met Cox, seem incompatible now and are likely "headed for the divorce courts." Kermit wants Malcolm to himself until Malcolm wonders whether Kermit is afraid of dying at his age, which prompts Kermit to call for Laureen. Laureen's comforting strokes arouse them both, and they send Malcolm away with exhortations to come back later, Kermit still vying for Malcolm's sole attention. Cox next sends Malcolm to the wealthy Girards, whom Malcolm hopes will know where his father is. The Girards are also on the verge of divorce, Madame Girard surrounded by young men and Girard Girard a "seducer of chambermaids and car hops." Madame Girard, resistant to Malcolm at first, ends by calling him a "true prince."

Madame Girard and her young men recall Mommy at the end of *The American Dream*, although Madame Girard's husband is still potent (consider also the "portrait of someone looks very much like you," 605). Laureen's warning about telling the secrets of a marriage to a third party (561, 563) recalls George's warning to Martha, and an argument over age (resonant with but more realistic than Laureen and Kermit's arguments over his age) will open *Three Tall Women*. *Malcolm* has minor resonances with *The Zoo Story* throughout. It opens with Malcolm on a bench and Cox making a second attempt to get Malcolm's attention. Cats, one named

Peter (566, cf. 19), are a feature of the Raphaelsons' marriage. To Malcolm's astonishment at the mention of his wife, Cox says, "Everybody is married" (568, cf. 17). To Madame Girard's "You may not have everything!!" Girard retorts, "Is that a rule, madame?" (603, cf. 35) Malcolm frequently says, "I don't understand" (559, 591, 603, 616; cf. 31-2), and Melba tickles Malcolm to distract him (622, cf. 33).

When Malcolm returns to tell Kermit about the Girards, he discovers that Laureen has left. Malcolm empathizes, "It's pretty scary, isn't it, being alone?" which prompts Malcolm to recall his father. Even though Kermit disparages Malcolm's father because "I wanted to talk about *my*self," Malcolm forgives him. And when Girard invites Malcolm to their chateau for the summer, because Madame Girard "has taken such an immediate and violent fancy to you," Malcolm refuses to go without Kermit. But Cox, who does not approve of what he hasn't arranged, gets to Kermit before Malcolm and crushes his spirit, reminding Kermit that he is one of Cox's students, all of "whom I've educated beyond your state, risen up so that you can look at life, if not in the eye, at least at the belt buckle." (Madame Girard refers to Cox as a pederast, 572-4.) Kermit, parroting Cox, rejects the Girards' invitation to the chateau on the grounds that he "can't bear the splendor." Malcolm, although feeling loss and rejection, is true to his word. Cox, who has evicted Malcolm from the hotel, advises Malcolm to "Start lower…ascend again" (note that George in *Woolf* says you can't "start back up once you're descending," 187), giving him another address.

Malcolm is next received by painter Eloisa Brace and her husband, ex-con and memoirist Jerome, who appreciates that Malcolm doesn't "seem to have any pre-judgments about anything." Jerome, like Madame Girard earlier, serves underage Malcolm drinks. Cox mentioned to Madame Girard that Eloisa was painting Malcolm's portrait; and now Madame Girard, who (although she considers Malcolm ungrateful) retains "for the boy—or, to put it most accurately, for the fact of him—a possessiveness that borders on mania," "will stop at nothing to have Malcolm's portrait." Madame Girard comes to the studio to demand the portrait and greets Malcolm with "Have you kept your innocence!" Girard follows, declaring that he will divorce Madame Girard, take her name from her, and marry Laureen Raphaelson. They exit seeking the Braces, leaving Malcolm alone with a sense of loss, craving his father. The Braces return to Malcolm, informing him that his portrait has been sold to Madame Girard and that he has been sold (at a little more than one-third of the cost of the portrait) to Girard Girard, whom he is to meet at the entrance to the botanical gardens.

II. Mature Him Up (*1CP 608-637*)

Malcolm, sleeping at the entrance to the botanical gardens, is awakened by Gus, on an errand to find a "contemporary" for his ex-wife Melba. Gus takes Malcolm to the club where Melba is performing, orders him a drink, and twice tells him to sit and wait (which resonates with *The Death of Bessie Smith*, except that Jack wanted to get in and Malcolm wants to get out). When Melba comes backstage, she says of Gus, "Six weeks of marriage teaches you an awful lot about a man," and suggests that Malcolm become her new husband, a union which will prove to be the culmination of Malcolm's "long short life." Melba requires that Gus "Mature him up a little" before she marries underage Malcolm, so Gus takes Malcolm to Rosita's, where the actor who plays Cox now plays another pander, Miles, who withdraws objections to Malcolm's age at the sight of Gus's money. Rosita says that Malcolm "has made an old woman very happy," and Malcolm, who takes a childish delight in making it "all the way through… three times," is whisked away by Melba to a Chicago wedding.

Melba drains the life from her new fifteen-year-old husband by denying him food, supplementing his alcohol with a substance that increases
his sexual activity, and making nightly appearances in clubs. When Malcolm uses a pet name that husband "number three called me," Melba is
caught off guard by the depth of feeling she normally denies and forbids
Malcolm to use the name (Melba-pussy) because "it's sacred." Malcolm is
struck too when he thinks he sees his father and rushes into the washroom
after him. Malcolm grapples desperately with the man, pleading "Please,
father! I've missed you so, and I've been so lonely," but the man violently
rejects Malcolm, throwing him to the floor hard enough to make his
head bleed. When an attendant (played by the actor who plays Cox but
not mistaken by Malcolm for Cox as Miles was) informs Malcolm, "That
couldn't have been you father, sonny," Malcolm gives up hope: "Maybe
he never existed at all!" (his doubt seeded earlier by Cox: "if your father
exists, or has ever existed," 569).

Girard Girard, who was late to the botanical gardens on "a business
matter of some urgency," begs Eloisa and Jerome for information on the
whereabouts of Malcolm but receives only indignation from Eloisa and
intimations of the "unimaginable [sexual] indignities of the cell block"
from Jerome. Madame Girard, now keeping company with Kermit, has
Malcolm's picture, but "It is *not* my Malcolm." She searches for "the one
decent thing in this entire world." Hearing the gossip concerning Malcolm's marriage, Madame Girard tracks Malcolm to Melba's solarium,
where a doctor informs them that Malcolm is "beyond human care,"
dying of alcoholism and "a violent protracted excess of sexual inter-
course." As Madame Girard comes to his bed, Malcolm, the perennial
innocent, can no longer face the reality of loss, asking, "[W]hat have I
not lost?" as he dies and the other characters enter his room. Madame
Girard's plea, "Did none of us ever care?" (which resonates with "All

we've *done* is think about ourselves" at the close of *All Over*, *2CP* 366) prompts ritual dispassion from all save Girard Girard, whose lament for Malcolm also serves as a lament for desire unrealized: "he passed through so quickly; none of us could grasp hold." Madame Girard notes that Malcolm's portrait is "all that's left" as lights crossfade to *"the golden bench, high on a platform, above and behind."*

Malcolm, like Jerry and *The American Dream*'s Young Man, is another of Albee's damaged children. He desires a father but is not offered one; his loneliness drives him to imagine he sees his father in a stranger who violently rejects him, leaving him to wonder whether his father ever existed. There are three sets of paired characters in *Malcolm*, all married. Arguments between these couples illustrate the influence of others on the shaping of our reality and identity. To Malcolm's query about whether Kermit and Laureen "can't both go on believing what they want" about how old Kermit really is, Cox replies, "Well, not if they're the only ones who believe it" (569). The Girards debate whether reality is defined by her detectives or his wits, and when Girard declares that he will give his wife the separation she has "demanded without cease since the melancholy day of our marriage," she retorts that she will "determine the relationship between what I wish and what I say I wish" and vows that he will never take her name from her (601-3).

Madame Girard's emotional monologue helps us see that she has come to truly care for Malcolm and adds the depth needed to bridge the gap between her buying Malcolm's portrait and arriving at his deathbed. In that final bedside scene, Albee uses simple repetitions of phrase to craft a brief but effective ritual. There are a couple of moments of attention to language here. Malcolm's addition of "like" into "Be *like* your son" prompts Girard's "Between simile and metaphor lies all the sadness in the world" (582), and Cox challenges Malcolm's word choices with "Guess!? Suppose!? You *know*!" (555) *Malcolm* has much in common structurally with another Albee adaptation, *Lolita* (and Malcolm becomes sexually active at an inappropriately young age like Lolita). They are his most episodic plays, and only *Lolita* comes close to using as many locations as *Malcolm*'s baker's dozen. Albee's previous episodic play, *The Ballad of the Sad Café*, another adaptation, needed only a unit set (316). *Malcolm* is the only play in which actors double as other characters; although in *Lolita* and *The Man Who Had Three Arms*, Albee calls for characters to impersonate other characters.

A DELICATE BALANCE

III. When the Daylight Comes Again

A Delicate Balance

Albee characterizes *A Delicate Balance* as concerning "the rigidity and ultimate paralysis which afflicts those who settle in too easily" (*2CP* 13-4) in 1996 and "a comfortable family invaded by reality long after they are capable of dealing with the invasion" (*2CP* 8) in 2004. Tobias and Agnes are invaded by the reality that their best friends of forty years, Harry and Edna, have become frightened and want to move in with them, a reality that threatens to tip their comfortable, settled lives out of balance.

I. Frightened and You Don't Know Why (*2CP* 19-48)

The characters in *A Delicate Balance* use drink to dull, language to distance, and settling to avoid the stark reality of fear common to the human experience. Drink offers are ubiquitous in this play. More drinks are discussed and poured here than in any Albee play, including

Who's Afraid of Virginia Woolf? (although here there are six characters drinking on three days rather than four characters drinking through one long night). The denial of fear is highlighted in the opening of the play, when Agnes, one of the most articulate of Albee's many articulate characters, says, "[A]side from my theoretically healthy fear—no, not fear, how silly of me—healthy speculation," in reference to the idea that she might lose her mind one day. Pausing to appreciate a partner's wit (as Agnes does with "Neat," 22) is a trait of many Albee couples, especially in *The Goat*. The sibling rivalry between Agnes and Claire is a precursor to that of the sisters in *Three Tall Women*. Agnes's takedown of Claire ("I apologize for being articulate," 25) prompts Claire to consider instigating an "occasion for another paragraph" and Tobias's "ineffectual stop-it-now's." Claire characterizes Tobias as "Predictable, stolid," and as having "indistinguishable if not necessarily similar friends" like Harry. When Claire suggests that Tobias needs a friend "to admit to that—now and then—you're suddenly frightened and you don't know why," Tobias denies, "Frightened? No." In reference to Claire's recounting of A.A. philosophy, Tobias echoes both George in *Woolf* and Cox in *Malcolm* with, "Once you drop...you can come back up part way...but never... really back again. Always...descent."

Of their daughter Julia's impending return home, Agnes says, "*I* don't want her here, God knows. I mean she's welcome, of course," foreshadowing Tobias's sentiment later to Harry. The gap between our desires and what we are offered is seen in the failure of Julia's four marriages and in the rejection of Tobias by his cat, who in contrast to Jerry's landlady's dog was successfully killed by Tobias's vet. An unsettling tone shift accompanies Harry and Edna's arrival, which was prompted by the fact that they were sitting home alone and got frightened, although "nothing at all happened." Harry's description recalls Julian after his marriage in *Tiny Alice*: "It was like being lost: very young again, with the dark, and lost." Claire predicts that Tobias will eventually know the reality of Harry and Edna's fear.

II. The Great Balancing Act (*2CP* 49-91)

The balance of routine can be threatened by family, but those threats will be managed (cf. Agnes on her ritual of comforting Julia, 85); this is not necessarily true for friends, whose burden is capable of disrupting the family routine. This act begins with Tobias asserting that Julia belongs at home (55) and ends with Edna claiming that she and Harry have more rights to be in the house than Julia and that "*We* belong" (88). Resonant with Cousin Lymon's sentiment about life on a chain gang in *Ballad* (cf. *1CP* 391), Agnes says, "It's one of those days when everything's underneath. But, we are all together… which is something." Agnes declares, "I shall…keep this family in shape. I shall maintain it; hold it." Claire asserts that Harry and Edna desire succor, comfort, and warmth from their friends but that "[w] e're not a communal nation…giving, but not sharing, outgoing, but not friendly." Julia sees Harry and Edna as usurping her room and wants "WHAT IS MINE!!"

The choice to settle rather than take risks in life is associated with a denial of reality or a loss of agency. Agnes speaks of a book with provocative ideas as one "to be read and disbelieved, for it disturbs our sense of well-being." Julia speaks of a period in her father's life when he was "nice but ineffectual," a "noneminence." Claire characterizes Tobias as having a "regulated great grey life." Agnes asserts that "nobody…*really* wants to talk about [Julia's] latest…marital disorder, really wants to talk *around* it." Claire says, "We submerge our truths and have our sunsets on untroubled waters." In contrast to these states of denial, Claire notes with acute sensitivity the differences in temperature and breathing rates in a house at night when people are sleeping versus when they are awake.

III. When the Daylight Comes Again (*2CP* 92-122)

Major decisions throughout the history of a relationship, like whether to conceive again after a child has died or whether to let Harry and Edna stay, are accompanied by the pressure of facing the sad reality of our inescapable self-concern. Agnes says, "We manufacture such a portion of our own despair…such busy folk." She characterizes Tobias as living in "dark sadness" and their lovemaking after their son Teddy's death as "Such…silent… sad, disgusted…love." Claire articulates the reality that Harry and Edna are making Tobias and Agnes face: "We have our friends and guests for patterns, don't we—known quantities.…We can't have changes—throws the balance off." Julia considers her godparents Harry and Edna to be intruders; Agnes characterizes them as "dear friends, our very best, [who] have come to us and brought the plague," a terror about which Agnes warns: "[I]f you are *not* immune, you risk infection." Tobias says that the decision is not an "abstract problem," but his unwillingness to ask them to leave is more about philosophy than about wanting them to stay. Tobias asks, "Doesn't forty years amount to anything?" He fears that if he dismisses Harry and Edna he is admitting that relationships, even relationships with his family, have no meaning, to which Agnes says, "Blood holds us together when we've no more…deep affection for ourselves than others." When Harry asks whether Tobias wants them there, Tobias replies, "You *came! Here!*"

Tobias, in conflict over his best friends' rights to their desires versus his own desires, unleashes "*all the horror and exuberance of a man who has kept his emotions under control too long*"—"BRING YOUR PLAGUE! YOU STAY WITH US! I DON'T WANT YOU HERE! I DON'T LOVE YOU! BUT

BY GOD…YOU STAY!!"—and characterizes his inability to offer more as
"my poverty." But Tobias's offer comes just after Harry's admission, "Toby,
I wouldn't let *you* stay." When Harry asks Edna whether Tobias and Agnes
love them, she says "Well…as much as we love them…I should think." Edna
realizes, "It's sad to come to the end of it" (A in *Three Tall Women* has the
opposite epiphany at the end of her play) and "still not have learned…the
boundaries, what we may not do…not ask, for fear of looking in a mirror
(Jerry feared this, too; cf. *1CP* 30). Edna laments "that the one body you've
wrapped your arms around…the only skin you've ever known…is your
own—and that it's dry…and not warm."

As Harry and Edna leave, Agnes offers a hollow "don't be strangers," to
which Edna replies, "[H]ow could we be? Our lives are…the same." Agnes
declines Edna's offer of a trip into town the following week with an equally
hollow "I've so much to do." This is just after Agnes laments how "[t]ime
happens" before we take action and how "[e]verything becomes…too late,
finally." Agnes uses the analogy of not going up a hill for a lack of action,
which resonates with imagery from the beginning of the play, where Agnes
comments on "how little I vary," noting "There are no mountains in my life…
nor chasms. It is a rolling, pleasant land" (22-3). The beginning of Agnes's
closing speech is almost identical to her opening speech. But now what she
finds astonishing, aside from the belief that she will one day lose her mind,
is not her irritation with Claire and Tobias's defense of Claire but rather "the
wonder of daylight": how "when the daylight comes again" it brings order,
assuaging our fear of darkness. She says, "Well, they're safely gone…and we'll
all forget…quite soon. (*Pause*) Come now; we can begin the day."

The strain of conflict on marriage or family bonds is a dominant theme
in this play. These bonds hold, though, whereas the bonds of friendship are
far more tenuous. As Edna says, "We mustn't press our luck, must we: test"

(117). Claire's commentary on her period of extreme drunkenness, which made her "more like an animal every day," reveals how desire and uncertainty affect our ability to face reality. She speaks of hating and of wanting love—"comfort and snuggling is what you really mean, of course" (31)—and says we love each other "to the depths of our self-pity and greed" (41). When an A.A. member praises her for taking a first step, she wonders what the step is toward: "Sanity, *in*sanity, revelation, self-deception" (33). Tobias, resistant to these raw revelations, asks when this period will be forgotten. Claire says, "When memory takes over and corrects fact" (31). In the immediate aftermath of the death of her son, Agnes denies the reality of her loss, doubting "that Teddy had ever lived at all" (80). Teddy's absence has a significant impact on his family.

Both sisters are conscious of language choices; Agnes substitutes "speculation" for "fear" (20), and Claire asks "Isn't ilk a lovely word?" (72). Claire insists that Tobias use a grammatically incorrect article (32-3). Agnes asserts that she is blessed with the meta-awareness "to view a situation objectively while I am in it" (67). Agnes makes what could be an unacknowledged theatrical reference to *Hedda Gabler* when she wishes Claire would kill herself "well, thoroughly" (34), although there's no suggestion that it be done beautifully. Claire refers to Julia as "Miss Julie" (63). There are several sequences of verbal virtuosity throughout the play: Agnes's intellectual musings (with interjections from Tobias) that open the play, her takedown of Claire (25), Claire's visceral revelations of sickness (31), the story of Tobias and the cat (with interjections from the sisters, 38-40), Tobias's *"aria"* (114), and Edna's coda that follows. Although it is structured climactically, there is a hint of circularity and ritual in Agnes's use of similar phrasing to begin and end the play. There are two sets of paired characters here, one *"very much like"* (17) the other. Agnes and Tobias's *"large and well-appointed suburban house"* (17) marks a return to a single, confined environment, as in *Who's Afraid of Virginia Woolf?*

EVERYTHING IN THE GARDEN

Pages   Outline
(*2CP*)

I. Forbidden Fruit (Act I, Scene 1)

127-134   A. I'm *trying* to save money
134-141   B. I just want to help
141-149   C. Money's hungry, lonely, wants more of itself
149-155   D. People can't just give people money
155-161   E. *I've* got some money

II. Temptation (Act I, Scene 2)

161-167   A. So proper; you'd never know
167-173   B. Well, open it
173-179   C. Do something wild
179-184   D. I won't say anything
184-191   E. It is for *us*; for everything we *want*
191-200   F. You *never* turn a clock back; *never*

III. Fall (Act II)

201-208   A. At each other's throats
208-219   B. A little knowledge is a dangerous thing
219-229   C. Things are going to be a little harder for *all* of us
229-236   D. How quickly you get used to the idea

Everything in the Garden

A lbee's adaptations of novels are quite faithful to their source material (but see Pease's contrast of Albee's *Malcolm* with Purdy's, and Grant's contrast of Albee's *Lolita* with Nabokov's; Pease 162-4, Grant 165-82), but for his adaptation of Giles Cooper's play, "barely a line of the source play [is] unaltered...leaving little more than the spine of Mr. Cooper's play intact" (*2CP* 7). This play is also unique in comparison to the rest of the Albee canon. Generally, the contradiction between desire and what we are offered implies a contradiction between a desired ideal and our inability to attain it. For Albee's characters, this is often a desire to be understood. Here, in Albee's bleakest play, a play that without the young teenager Roger would be devoid of hope, the characters are concerned only with satisfying their petty, materialistic desires. When offered the temptation to satisfy those desires, "the isolation of money" (174) exacerbates their baseness and self-absorption, and they fall into a "savage" reality (241), one in which they are indignant and retaliatory to the teenager who challenges their racism and to the point of murdering someone who might expose their criminal greed.

I. Forbidden Fruit (*2CP* 127-161)

Richard and Jenny argue about the costs that contribute to their strained financial situation, lamenting the need to smoke cheap, bad cigarettes without ever considering that they could choose to quit smoking. Richard articulates the absurdity of the logic that has landed them in this situation:

> You live in a forty-thousand dollar house and you have to smoke bad cigarettes to get the coupons so you can afford a good vacuum so you can clean it; you belong to the club so you can pay back dinner invitations from people you wouldn't even know if you hadn't joined the club in the first place, and you *joined* the club, *and* learned how to play tennis, because you decided to move into a neighborhood where everybody belonged to the club. (135)

Jenny's response to this is "Except the Jews and the tradespeople." When Richard asks why they pursue this course, Jenny says, "[B]ecause we want to live nicely." Earlier Richard had characterized it as trying to live like the friends they didn't have until they moved. He says, "I don't feel I belong anywhere."

In addition to the racism and elitism of Jenny, Richard, and their friends, there is also an environment of sexism in the play. Richard refuses to allow Jenny to apply for a job. When she says "You think I'm worthless," he jokes "I imagine I could sell you," foreshadowing the fact that Jenny will soon sell herself. While Jack is concerned enough for Richard and Jenny to decide secretly to leave them his money, he says, "I'd do almost anything for you....Unless it got in the way of what I wanted to do for me." And Jenny is primarily an object to Jack. In his first address to the audience he says, "Jenny is…good. Damn it; wish she weren't." His propositions aren't really jokes, which prompts Jenny's assertion to Mrs. Toothe that Jack's joking claims of intimacy with her are false. Jack does dispense wise advice about money, though: "Money's hungry, lonely, wants more of itself." Even after Jack's warning about money and Jenny's initial indignant shock at Mrs. Toothe's offer to employ her as a prostitute, the revelation that one of Jenny's friends is secretly employed by Mrs. Toothe tempts her to use the money advanced to her by Mrs. Toothe. Jenny claims that her refusal of Jack's offer to paint her portrait is because she wants "to be different" than all the women Jack paints, but her refusal also supports her opposition to introspection: "I just don't want to look at myself, that's all."

II. Temptation (*2CP* 161-200)

Six months into Jenny's new occupation, Richard speaks disparagingly of a promiscuous woman he knew to contrast her with Jenny, just before it is revealed that Jenny too is "[s]o proper; you'd never know." Jenny considers her job to be as dull as Richard's. She says that the money "is for *us*; for everything we *want*" and that what she does "doesn't make any difference to *us*," prompting Richard to slap her twice. Jenny "*slaps him back, just as hard as he hit her*," another instance of marital violence in Albee's work. Tickling as provocation (166), the idea of not confusing the symbol with the thing itself (182), and quibbles over a character's age (137, 163, 217) recur here, too. Money has imbued Jenny with status and confidence; she exhibits strength and determination upon her son Roger's entrance just after the slaps and through her insistence that Richard prepare for the guests she's just invited over, even as he falls apart under the weight of his new knowledge.

III. Fall (*2CP 201-256*)

Money gives Jenny the sense that she is powerful and that she can share that power with Richard. When Roger asks if Richard was about to hit her, Jenny says, "[Y]our father doesn't hit people bigger than he is." She suggests that Richard might be able to look their friends in the eye now and "talk about the new car you're going to get, and why don't we raise the dues at the club to keep the riffraff out." Jenny defends her prostitution with a blistering castigation of the immoralities associated with Richard's job and the jobs of their friends: "[Y]ou're all killers and whores." Their friends are even more shallow and self-focused than Richard and Jenny. When Roger calls out Gilbert's use of a racist epithet, Gilbert asks Richard, "What did I say?" Richard, embarrassed by his son's inability to let another racist remark go without comment, says, "You're not fit to associate with decent people," which denies the reality of Roger's moral fitness and of Richard's friends' indecency.

When Mrs. Toothe enters to inform Jenny that a police detective has told her "to clear out," she finds that all her "suburban ladies" happen to be under one roof, and the quartet of couples also discover their mutual secret. Mrs. Toothe prepares to make a business proposition, sending the women to the garden so that it can be "talked about amongst us men." Her money, obtained by preying on the desires of men for sex and of women for the status that only money can bring in a sexist environment, allows her to dictate terms and usurp Richard's authority in his home. (As it did for Tobias, the usurpation of Richard's role as bartender (226) also signals his loss of authority. There is a good bit of drinking in this play, but it seems tame in comparison to *A Delicate Balance*.) Mrs. Toothe proposes that she move her operation into Richard and Jenny's neighborhood. Richard's acquiescence, his fall, like Julian's in *Tiny Alice*, makes him feel like a lost little boy (235). Jack enters and brings news of the ousting from the club of a couple discovered to be Jewish. Jack mocks the guests' indignant shock that the ousted wife "never let *on*" with a fitting reality check: "For God's sake, you'd think she was a common prostitute." Richard exercises the only authority he has left by bullying Roger into reciting the Ten Commandments, of which Roger recalls only "Thou shalt not kill." After Roger is sent to his room, the decent people proceed to kill Jack after he discovers their secret. At Mrs. Toothe's urging, the men bury Jack in the garden. Recognizing the trauma this immorality will cause the men, she urges the women to comfort their husbands: "You'll have to be the strong ones…as usual." Louise says, "At least it wasn't…one of us. I mean, someone, well…with a family, someone…regular."

All of the adult characters are self-concerned (Jack admittedly so), lack awareness, and resist facing reality. Richard's sarcasm is "*not seen*" by the guests. Immediately after killing Jack, Chuck says, "We didn't do that." Jenny denies that she said Jack would talk, but is reminded by Mrs. Toothe, "You said he would talk. You agreed he would." Mrs. Toothe even urges the other characters to face reality in order to deny reality. After Jack's murder, she asserts that "something *has* happened" and that "[y]ou can't go *back*" (cf. "You *never* turn a clock back; *never*," 197). "You make the best as you go on," even though, like with our face lifts, our false faces, "we convince…some people…but we don't believe it ourselves" (251). Even so, Mrs. Toothe assures Jenny and Richard that soon "everything in the garden…will be as it was." Like Grandma, Jack comes back in unseen by the other characters to talk to the audience:

"It's amazing how dying sobers you up." Jack's disappearance means "it'll be seven years until I can be declared officially dead," so Richard and Jenny will have to wait to inherit Jack's houses and his millions. Jack wonders if they can live with what they've done that long. Jenny asserts that if people let their gardens go "you know there's something wrong in the house" and suggests that Mrs. Toothe's new garden should be "kept up. I think it should look like all the others." Richard immediately complies. Jack says, "I think they'll make it."

Albee's usual themes are somewhat inverted in this play. There is family conflict, but the bonds, primarily financial, are shallow. Identity is shaped by a surface comparison to others' material possessions rather than by a need to be understood, although Richard does have an introspective moment when he says, "I don't feel I belong anywhere" (136). Richard and Jenny have a potential for self-awareness that the other couples do not have, but they choose not to rise to that potential. Mrs. Toothe is especially insidious in her assistance of their denials. She soothes Richard's rage at his supplication with "One can forget. If something isn't good to live with, or convenient, one can forget. After all, there are things you *have* to forget if you want to live at all" (234). Mrs. Toothe perverts the ideal of facing stark reality in coaching the couples on how to live with their murder of Jack. Although Roger is neglected and mistreated, he is perhaps the least damaged of Albee's young men and provides a moral contrast to the adults in the play.

Linguistically, Richard struggles for correct phrasing (135); Richard and Jenny both correct "imply"/"infer" usage (137-9); Roger privately makes singular Perry's plural "folks" (215-6); and Jack amends "by the club" to "*at* the club" (237). As madam Toothe proposes bringing love in the afternoon into the couples' neighborhood, Roger notes that the "sun isn't even down yet" but "Venus is up," and Mrs. Toothe asks Richard if he has "an objection to my…wetting my lips in your house" (223, 225). So far only one character at a time has addressed the audience in an Albee play, but Albee suggests that it "*might be interesting*" if Richard "*looked the people in the audience right in the eye*," but without becoming a second speaker, without an "*attempt to set a new convention*" (201). Albee will have two (or more) people speak to the audience in future plays. Albee continues to acknowledge the uniqueness of individual performances in his stage directions: Richard "*Goes to—what? a side table, maybe*" (184), and Jack shushes the audience "*whether necessary or not*" (253). Richard chooses to characterize Jenny's most honest statement in the play as theatrics: "That's quite a performance" (206; cf. George to Martha (*1CP* 289) and Jack to Gillian, *3CP* 279). Albee characterizes the trio of couples who attend Richard and Jenny's party as "*very much like*" them (126). Names are not abstracted, but there is some playfulness with the serpentine Toothe and the nature of Cyn. The characters' sense of confinement is caught in Jenny's response to Richard's protest that there are other standards than money: "Not in *our* environment" (205). Structurally, the play is climactic, even though it is necessary for six months to pass between the first two scenes to establish the solidity of Jenny's new status. Albee's plays to this point have not strayed far from traditional theatrical structures and conventions. His next two inter-related plays will be two of the most experimental in the Albee canon.

BOX and QUOTATIONS FROM CHAIRMAN MAO TSE-TUNG

III. Box (Reprise)

Box and Quotations from Chairman Mao Tse-tung

I n his introduction to these plays, Albee describes *Mao* as "an out-growth of and extension of" *Box* and both plays as experiments "with the application of musical form to dramatic structure." Albee articulates his obligations as a playwright—attempts "to alter his society" and "to alter [dramatic] forms"—and the obligation of the audience "to experience a work on its own terms" (*2CP* 261-2). *Box* is a distillation of Albee's concern with our lost potential; *Mao* a distillation of Albee's concern with our isolation and distance from reality.

I. Box (*2CP* 263-267)

Voice admires the well-constructed, beautiful box and laments that we are "corrupt to the selfishness," that we are capable—"That it *can* be *done* is the crack," the flaw in the construction—of "spilling and spilling [pounds of milk] and killing all those children ["Seven hundred million babies"] to make a point," a loss of humanity and human potential so large that "the momentum is too much": we are unable to countenance it save symbolically.

Music is one of the "arts which have gone down to craft." "When art begins to hurt"; when music makes you "cry from loss"; when it is "a reminder! And not of what *can*...but what *has*"; "When the beauty of it reminds us of *loss*. Instead of the attainable. When it tells us what we cannot have...well, then...it no longer relates...*does* it." "When art hurts," "Then the corruption is complete," and "Nothing belongs." When "you can't come back; when you get in some distant key" there is no "release of tension," no "return to consonance." Alternately, "the beauty of art is order—not what is familiar, necessarily, but order...on its own terms," when "one comes back, not circular, not to the starting point, but a...setting down again." Art is anticipation, potential, the "memory of what we have not known," the unheard but known "resolution of a chord," what "can happen" but is "unprovable." And the artist is the "one below" the sky of birds, "moving fast in the opposite way," giving the flock an awareness of its potential for change, of the potential for beauty and order in the unfamiliar.

II. Quotations from Chairman Mao Tse-tung (*2CP* 268-297)

Voice from *Box* joins a quartet of isolated characters in *Quotations from Chairman Mao Tse-Tung*. In his opening comments to the latter play, Albee says, "Primarily the characters must seem interested in what they themselves are doing and saying." He gives meticulous notes about the range of their interactions and movements:

	Relation to Audience	Relation to Other Characters	Movement
Mao	always speaks to	aware, doesn't look at, speech not influenced by	may wander a little
Long-Winded Lady	never speaks to	speaks to Minister	stays at deck chair
Old Woman	speaks only to	aware, may look at, speech not influenced by	stays in one place, up
Minister (no lines)	doesn't look at	LWL only	stays in deck chair

The narrative rhythms of the speaking characters are widely varied: Mao speaks from his writings *"rather like a teacher"*; Old Woman is *"reciting a poem"*; and Long-Winded Lady is so conscientious of what she says that she often seems to be rambling. All of these characters speak in an inviting rhythm crafted for listeners but without the expectation of a verbal response, their speech therefore much like music. The lack of character interaction creates a sense of isolation or distance in contrast to those conversational rhythms.

Albee's arrangement of the three unrelated texts—Mao's, Carleton's for the Old Woman, and his for the Long-Winded Lady—was "governed by a sense of musical composition" (Gussow 274, cf. Solomon 109) and clearly with an ear toward thematic unity as well (cf. the outline above), highlighting the common ideas shared by varied personalities, regardless of their mutual isolation. Both Long-Winded Lady and the narrator of Carleton's poem recited by Old Woman are widows who have strained relationships with their children. The narrator of the poem experiences the shock and betrayal of being put in the poor house by her child. Long-Winded Lady feels betrayed by her husband's death and her daughter's attitude toward her. Her narrative is centered in the shocking experience of falling overboard and its aftermath. Mao believes the Chinese people are betrayed by imperialism; and while the overthrow of imperialism will be a shock, he believes it to be inevitable and to require violent action. As indicated in the outline above, the play progresses through a military-style sequence driven by Mao but always resonant with the other speaking characters. For each, there is comprehension of an important idea or event, an assertion of the will to take action, and a lament for, or consideration of, actions given depth by historical context. The narratives of politics, war, death, and filial relations all feature aggression, marked boundaries, surprise attacks, opposed forces, and turns of dominance and submission, narratives that, as common denominators of human experience, tend to corruption rather than completion.

Another common human tendency is to distance or to manipulate the reality of experience. Long-Winded Lady usually speaks of her fall from the perspective of an outside observer. She "manufactured the pain" of her broken thumb before "the hurt could have come through. I made it happen" (274). Speaking of an accident that she at first thought was staged for film, she says, "One…concludes things—and if those things and what is really there don't…are not the *same*…well!… it would usually be better if it were so. The mind does that: it helps" (276). Her husband's violent dying and his small stature resonate with the husband of *Three Tall Women*. Her distinction between dying and death, her self-concern ("WHAT ABOUT ME!"), her statement "his dying is all over" (287-8), and her conflict with her daughter lead directly into Albee's next play, *All Over*. The reality of dying is more visceral than the abstraction of death, an abstraction that allows Mao to speak clinically and persuasively of war ("politics with bloodshed," 294) as a necessary condition to achieve peace. In general, one can die for a cause, but specifically, the Long-Winded Lady says, "*I have nothing to die for*" (297).

III. Box (Reprise) (*2CP* 298-299)

In the wake of the isolation and distance from reality associated with the characters of *Mao*, there are notable excisions in the reprise of *Box*. (Albee cut even more of this text in a production he directed, cf. Solomon 106.) Voice does not speak of the box's fine construction or the room inside it, contributing to a greater sense of inattention and confinement in the reprise. There is no mention of milk, the last word spoken by Voice in *Mao*. But although spilled milk may be ignored, it "does not unspill" (265), just as the murdered children associated with the milk do not come back to life. There is no discussion of the tonic necessary to relieve artistic tension, but Voice does still speak of "the resolution of a chord" and "the memory of what I'll not prove" and the lone bird "moving beneath…in the opposite way."

In *Box*, the reality is that beauty reminds us of loss, and the play is a paean to lost potential. In *Mao*, Long-Winded Lady is adept at keeping reality at a distance. She speaks of "the sound I imagine someone else would have manufactured had *he* been there" when she went overboard. Of the accident she witnessed, she says "It was real death, and real glass, and the fire, and the…people crying, and the crowds and the smoke. Oh, it was real enough, but it took me time to know it. The mind does that." She speaks more about the sound her fall made than about the experience of the fall. She relishes her experience of eating the food she was carrying when she saw the accident rather than dwelling on the "carnage" of the accident: "glass all over and…confusion." She at first remembers what she ate as "crullers" rather than the doughnut "hearts…pinched out, or cut" that are more resonant with the imagery of the accident (276-9). She says she'll "not touch" her husband's dying again, characterizing it as "long, course, and ugly," turning him into "a beast" (287). In addition to associating the reality of dying with animal nature, she characterizes adult screams as "animal protest" (274); Mao disdains reactionaries as "paper tigers," (279). Long-Winded Lady engages in contests of silence with her daughter rather than asking her what makes her happy (291). The realization before her fall that there is no railing is "as sudden and sure as what you've always known and never quite admitted to yourself" (293). Her questioners not knowing "who Trollope was" prompts a rumination: "You lead a whole life;… you write books, or you do not, and you say your name is Trollope… or whatever it may be, no matter what, you say your name…and they have…never…heard of it" (296). This lament for lost identity resonates in Voice's "Nothing belongs" (299).

Mao and Old Woman speak directly to the audience, Old Woman reciting someone else's text. Long-Winded Lady often describes her experience as if looking on it from outside. Albee again acknowledges a range of potential choices in his stage directions, using the qualifier "*If a thin actor is playing the role*" in his description of the Minister and suggesting that "*Perhaps*" the figures from *Mao* are kept in silhouette for the reprise of *Box*. The measured silences in *Box* and the repetition of the text of *Box* in *Mao* and *Box (Reprise)* give these plays a ritual quality. *Mao*, the rhythms of which will be "self-evident" in "an out-loud reading" (270), also features repetitions from Old Woman and Long-Winded Lady. All the characters in the pair of plays have abstracted names, save Mao, and all the speeches in the plays are monologues, broken up and arranged in turn-taking sequence by Albee. Voice envelops the audience, the sound coming "*from the back or the sides of the theatre.*" Although there is "room enough to walk around in" the box, there is a sense of confinement and limitation in that the box takes up "*almost all of a small stage opening*" and in Voice's characterization of "System as conclusion, in the sense of method as an end, the dice so big you can hardly throw them anymore" (264). The set for *Mao* "*appears within the outlines of the cube.*" These plays are Albee's most experimental structurally and center on themes of loss and isolation. The imagery of *Box* gains depth with each repetition. As Voice says, "[O]ne comes back, not circular, not to the starting point, but a...setting down again."

ALL OVER

All Over

Albee's discernment between the abstraction of death and the concrete, visceral act of dying was introduced in *Tiny Alice* and *Mao*. While *All Over* is structured around that concept, the play is more concerned with what Albee calls "closing down," characterized here primarily as retreat from another person.

I. Dying (*2CP* 305-334)

Although his immediate family, mistress, best friend, doctor, and nurse have gathered around the dying man, the gathered are for the most part more self-concerned than supportive of each other. There are several examples of our inability to reach each other along the spectrum from disconnection to hostility. The Wife (beginning with *All Over*, Albee places articles before the abstracted names of his characters in the speech headings) describes how, in a conversation with her husband, his "eyes went out—stayed open, went out." The Mistress corroborates that it "happened often": "an indication that…some small fraction had gone out of him, some…faint shift from total engagement." Of his relationship with his wife just before he had her committed, The Best Friend says, "I watched myself withdraw, step back and close down" (310-2). These withdrawals have reciprocal effects. The Mistress speaks of "the tiniest betrayal":

> THE MISTRESS:…it can be anything, or nearly nothing, except that it moves you back into yourself a little, the knowledge that all your sharing has been…
> THE WIFE:…arbitrary…
> THE MISTRESS:…willful, and that nothing has been inevitable…or even necessary. When the eyes close down; go out. (312-3)

The Wife prefers infidelity to divorce and equates the isolation (the "leave *alone*") of divorce with murder. The Best Friend recounts that when he asked his ex-wife, on the one occasion he saw her after the divorce, how she was, she replied, "It's fine in here…how is it out there?" He says, "I was so aware of her eyes on me, and her sister's." Rather than facing eyes that have gone out or closed down, The Best Friend faces hostile or "mad eyes." Rather than come to grips with the discomforting reality of the situation, "what I retain of their leaving" is "her sister's bracelet clanking against the steering wheel" (322-4).

Dying is correlated with isolation and denial. The Doctor says of his work with death-row inmates that "they were alone in the death cells, no access to each other" (321). The Nurse tells of a man who, dying of cancer, decides to go to his lodge and fish for a week before killing himself. The fiction, "invented by his wife and agreed to by his mistress," that he went down on the Titanic, although not believed, "became a euphemism and was eventually accepted" (319). The acknowledgement of our dying and our love as being essential to life could bridge our distances, but we deny these opportunities. One Christmas Eve, The Mistress, aware that the dying man missed his family, encouraged him to spend the holiday with them. "He said he thought not, and it was not for *my* sake." Speaking of public figures, The Nurse characterizes "the act of dying" as something the public craves to share in as opposed to simply reading about "merely the death" after the fact (327-8). The Wife laments that "*you* love yourself so little" to her daughter, but does so in a blistering, hostile speech (329). Both The Mistress and The Wife confront The Daughter with harsh truths, but The Daughter, underneath all her unpleasantness, craves her mother's affection. She asks, "Does *anyone* love me?" to which her mother, who is aggressively unsympathetic to her children throughout the play, responds, "Do *you* love anyone?" It was the same response The Wife at age nine or ten gave to the same question asked by her aunt, who would die in a car crash at 62 but who "died in the heart" at 26 (333).

II. Death (*2CP* 335-366)

Harsh truths continue to be asserted, but not lovingly. The Best Friend is matter-of-fact and cold with The Son (337). The Mistress warns The Daughter about how her self-possession will lead to an inability to express love, but she does so in hostile fashion, ignoring her own advice: "You lash out—which can be a virtue…if it's used to protect and not just as revenge" (339). After being cruel to her brother (340), The Daughter defends him against cruelty from their mother, but only after he has left the room (349-50).

The Wife characterizes herself as "a symbol of stability rather than refuge" to her husband, in contrast to The Mistress, who then tells a story of her first love reminiscent of Jerry's (352, cf. *1CP* 24). Albee's characters frequently express their desire to be understood, and here The Daughter and The Mistress both characterize themselves as misunderstood (335, 355). The Wife's account of her first meeting with her future husband (362-3) foreshadows a similar account in *Three Tall Women*. Both The Wife and The Mistress are articulate about the reality of what they'll do without the dying man. The Mistress doesn't want to be like the widows returning to shared places and facing "all the things they have come there to not admit." The Wife contemplates no change but realizes she might be lying to herself and have "no idea what I'm storing up." "Anger, resentment, loss, self-pity—*and* self-loathing—loneliness. You can't live with all that in the consciousness very long, so you put it under, *or* it gets well, and you're never sure which" (360-1). When the news comes that the death is occurring, The Wife does indeed break down and lash out, telling all but The Doctor and The Nurse that she doesn't love them, and "*[i]t explodes from her, finally, all that has been pent up for thirty years.*" The Wife realizes in the end that "[a]ll we've *done* is think about ourselves" (366), but does The Wife, who has just ordered her son to stop sobbing, correlate her assertion of that truth with the painful, sobbing assertion of her unhappiness that follows it?

The Wife and The Mistress protect the dying man from the press with "*an animal fury*" (334), and The Mistress warns The Daughter about only being able to express love and need with "the snarl of a wounded and wounding animal" (339). The Wife asserts that it was divorce that sent The Best Friend's ex-wife, who sees a mouse chewing into her ex-husband's ear, "spinning back into the animal brain" (322). While still in the hospital, the dying man's tubes and wires make him appear to be "an octopus" (308). The people waiting outside are described as "the kind of crowd you'd get for a horse with sunstroke" (327). The Wife's animal bond with her children has long since deteriorated into pure conflict: "I would have killed for my children, back when I cared for them" (361). To The Wife's harsh taunt about facing his father's dying—"Aren't you up to it?"—The Son counters "Not up to you, mother; never was" (349-50).

The play begins with a linguistic quibble over verb tense. When The Daughter mocks the The Mistress for this, The Wife chastises, "Semantics from a C minus?" (305, 311) The Mistress later calls The Daughter "imprecise" (342). Albee again acknowledges a variety of choices in his character and set descriptions and with the use of "*perhaps*" in his stage directions (335, 362). His use of "*fruity*" (321, 342) in his 1971 stage directions is insensitive by our standards, but Albee didn't change the description for the play's inclusion in the 2005 collection. The monologue experiment of *Mao* influences Albee's crafting of a realistic play that is more dependent on monologue than most of his previous work. The majority of monologues in subsequent plays will be spoken by characters who acknowledge the presence of an audience, often addressing the monologues to the audience. The Mistress speaks of holiday and funeral rituals (325, 343), but while the gathering of these characters for the unseen patriarch's dying is ritualistic, the play's only structural sense of ritual is in the repetitions of "the little girl I was when he came to me" (beginning on 314) and in the repetitions and tableau that close the play. In *All Over*, all character names are abstracted for the first time since *The Sandbox* and *Fam and Yam*, but Albee will make this choice for several of the plays that follow. There is an environmental shift between the acts from "*waiting*" to "*a dream state*." Sandwiched between the structural experiments of *Box Mao Box* and *Listening* and *Counting the Ways* are two standard climactic plays in familiar Albee locales: *All Over* occurs in a confined room; *Seascape* occurs on a beach, albeit a beach visited by anthropomorphic lizards.

SEASCAPE

Seascape

Seascape articulates Albee's stance against closing down and settling as opposed to living life to its fullest. Charlie resists Nancy's exhortations to explore new ground with a defeatist "What's to be gained?" which recalls Jerry's reflection on his attempt to communicate with the dog: "[W]hat is gained is loss" (*1CP* 31). Leslie, too, resists Nancy's assertion of the inevitability of his and Sarah's ascent with "Do we *have* to?"

I. What's To Be Gained? (*2CP* 371-399)

Nancy believes that the gap between desire and the attainable can be bridged, that a truer reality lies underneath our fear and loss: "[F]igure out what you'd really like—what you want without knowing it, what would secretly please you, put it in your mind, then make all the plans." To Charlie's assertion that he's "happy doing nothing,"

135

Nancy chides, "[I]s that what we've...come all this way for?...To lie back down in the crib again? The same at the end as at the beginning? Sleep? Pacifier? Milk? Incomprehensible once more?" (374) As in *Box*, milk, like art that hurts, is a reminder of loss: "not of what *can*...but what *has*" (265; also resonant with *Box* is Sarah's wonder at seagulls, 427). Her desire undaunted by Charlie's inertia, Nancy suggests, "Let's merely have it for today...: continue the temporary and it becomes forever" (376). In another effort to encourage Charlie's liveliness, Nancy suggests that he "reconfirm" the treasured underwater experiences of his youth, to which he counters, "I'd rather remember" (380). Nancy's goad of "All closed down?" is met with "There's comfort in settling in" (391). In contrast to Charlie's submissive nature and his view of Leslie and Sarah as a threat, Nancy's "submission" (399) pose is an active effort to reach them: "They're magnificent!" (395)

II. Do We *Have* To? (*2CP 400-448*)

At first, Charlie would rather assume he is dead than face the wonder of "Great...green...creatures coming up from the sea" (411). Nancy chides, "I mean, we *have* to be dead, because Charlie has decided that the wonders do not occur; that what we have not known does not exist; that what we cannot fathom cannot be; that the miracles, if you will, are bedtime stories" (430). After an interspecies conversation concerning commonalities, differences, instinct, and the nature of existence, and after Sarah articulates "a sense of not belonging" under the sea any more, Charlie exhorts Leslie and Sarah to stay: "I don't know what I feel toward you; it's either love or loathing. Take your pick; they're both emotions....I want you to know about *all* of it; I'm impatient for you. I want you to experience the whole thing!" (443) Jerry says to Peter, "We neither love nor hurt because we do not try to reach each other" (*1CP* 31). The Wife in *All Over* loves and hurts her children, but her impulse is to make them face an ugly reality that she defines, and her reach is a slap or an order. Charlie and Nancy offer to help Leslie and Sarah experience what they consider to be an inevitable reality, to take them by the hand (448), to reach fellow creatures descended from common ancestors. The optimism of the closing line in this play, Leslie's "Begin," retains a hint of threat (cf. *SMM* 287) and stands in contrast to the finality of the previous play's closing line ("All over") and to Agnes's use of "begin the day" (122) to close *A Delicate Balance* with an exhortation to forget.

Albee says that "*Seascape* wonders whether we are an evolving species or perhaps a devolving one. Two lizards; two humans" (*2CP* 9). The play includes discussion about animal behavior and instinct and images of fish and birds. Charlie and Nancy end the first act in a canine submission pose. Charlie says that tools, art, and mortality are "what separate *us* from the brute beast" (442). For many of Albee's characters, facing reality means facing their mortality, but Charlie fears life more than death (433). He says that his childhood immersions were a game, that they weren't "*real*" (436), but then admits of his motives toward educating Leslie and Sarah: "Maybe I envy you…down *there*, free from it all; down there with the *beasts*" (443).

We must shed our illusions to face stark reality. But theoretically our existence might be illusory (431). Words can be lies that we use to hide what we want without knowing it (390, 374), and we allow our closing down to become our reality. The way up from this is to choose wonder over reality, which requires facing extreme difference: "[I]f the differences are too extreme…well, then, reality tends to fade away" (426). Leslie and Sarah's urge to come up is tied to their identity:

"[W]e didn't feel we *belonged* there anymore" (437). The couples of both species have a strong bond. Minor conflict occurs when Nancy urges Charlie to life, but Nancy quells his fear of life with a passionate kiss (433). Nancy recounts only one dark time, when she was "learning the moles on your back instead of your chest hairs" (381). Nancy's mother passes on the wisdom of striving for compassion even in the face of the stark reality of an intimate betrayal. If you realize your husband imagines another woman as he touches you, "then you'll know something about loneliness, my daughter; yessiree; you'll be halfway there, halfway to compassion....Knowing how lonely *he* is" (383).

The play's title is both a contrast to landscape and a merger of sea escape. Nancy takes pride in a witticism, saying, "[N]ice, isn't it, when the real and the figurative come together" (383), and chides Charlie for saying she has had (instead of is having) a good life (389). Albee again uses "very much like," here to compare human and whale mammaries. Leslie chides Nancy for the "imprecision" of the word "emotions" (419). Three French playwrights (378) and Proust (381-2) are referenced in the play. Nancy and Charlie respond ritually each of three times a plane passes over the beach (371, 376, 434). Albee gives both Charlie and Nancy rich monologues (378-83), but there are no monologues in the interspecies dialogue of Act Two. *Seascape* is one of three Albee plays set on a beach, and one of about one-third of Albee's plays that features multiple paired couples. Like almost two-thirds of Albee's plays, *Seascape* is structurally climactic. Albee's next two plays are unique in that he makes their structural division explicit to his audience.

LISTENING

II. *I* Listen

Listening

As in *All Over*, closing down in *Listening* is represented by retreat from another person. We assume that if we have a listener, we are making contact with another person; but one can listen without paying attention, without responding to the reach of another. Relationships in *Listening* are kept at a distance, and personal connection is relegated to memory or denied or withheld.

I. You Don't *Listen* (*2CP* 453-484)

Listening begins with The Man's lament that the former garden (now overgrown) and the lavish, empty fountain pool to which he has been called have "become…impersonal" (453). And so has The Woman who called him there; she refuses to acknowledge their former intimacy, abstracting her personal experiences into generalized memories. To The Man's "You *did* hold my hand" she says, "*I've* held everybody's hand.…And, *did* I? *Did*

I hold your hand?" (455) The Man, talking to himself after The Woman goes to retrieve her charge The Girl, decides that they did hold hands. Although The Man makes a quintuple claim that the garden and the fountain are "Very much" as expected, there is a gap between The Man's desire for the grandeur and intimacy of the past and what is offered by the garden, the fountain, and The Woman now. *Listening* is the most menacing and mysterious of Albee's plays since *Tiny Alice*, and there are a few minor resonances with *Tiny Alice* here. The Man wonders whether the wall and fountain were "brought over—stone by stone" (453; cf. *1CP* 480); there may be a skeleton of a "mouse" in the fountain (468); The Girl asserts the significance of a "model" (476-7); and The Woman uses the phrase "what we believe" (488, 489).

Upon entering with The Woman, The Girl sits by the empty pool and, like The Man, craves The Woman's attention. The Man, an "institutional cook" (497), attempts to engage The Girl in conversation with "I do your food," but The Girl withdraws *"into herself"* (461-2). The Woman, in a mysterious exchange, forces The Man to recant his assertion that he doesn't care what The Woman does, before The Woman forces The Girl into conversation by snapping her fingers. The following ritual exchange between The Girl and The Woman occurs throughout the play:

> THE GIRL: You don't *listen*.
> THE WOMAN: . . . Well, that may *be*.
> THE GIRL: Pay attention, rather, is what you don't do. (464)

This exchange between The Woman and The Girl occurs again in beats seven, nine, eleven, and thirteen (Albee does not use headers as he usually does to indicate division of the text into scenes; rather, The Voice announces each beat of the undivided text in numerical sequence).

Alternately, beats eight, ten, and twelve feature tense exchanges between The Woman and The Man.

In their first exchange (which sets up their final exchange), The Woman says she'd know if The Girl found sharp glass in the fountain because "I can hear your pupils widen." The Girl's questions about the fountain—who built it, is it ever filled up, why is there no water—resonate with The Man's longing for a richer past. The Woman consistently introduces uncertainty to thwart comforting resolutions. She says that she used to come to the fountain a "long time ago" but won't reveal whether the fountain was filled, and responds to The Girl's "Who are *you*?" with "Who *am* I?" After implying intimacy with The Man (472), she chastises both her listeners for assuming the person who accompanied her to the fountain in the past was The Man (479) and does not answer The Man's eight questions about the fountain and her escort (481-2).

The Woman rebukes The Girl for hitting another of her charges: "You're not the only one with a couple of problems. Learn to look around you." The Girl's defense is that the other girl was stealing special "cardboard taken and made blue, self-made." When The Woman challenges the cardboard's self-made status, The Girl insists, "It was the model; it was the blue from which I would have made my own." The Woman says that the other girl cried tears of "sadness in the face of beauty" over the blue cardboard and asks The Girl, "What if *she* had hit *you*? *Back*, I mean?" without the possibility of intervention from the staff. At the suggestion of this unmediated, visceral contact with another person, The Girl becomes unresponsive, staring into the empty pool.

II. *I* Listen (*2CP 484-518*)

The Woman's grandmother, "not long before she died," said, "[T]he greatest sin in living is doing it badly—stupidly, or as if you weren't really alive" (489). But our self-concern ("we all love ourselves," 501), which prompts insecurity and isolation, is a ubiquitous obstacle to being really alive, which carries with it an openness to risk, to connection with other people. In her frustration, The Woman says "Everything scares us—prolapse, blood, the heartbeat…Why live!?" (514); but The Woman, who seems to judge The Girl for isolating herself, deftly keeps others at a distance by generating uncertainties, by listening in order to pick apart with questions rather than to bond. As The Woman tells the story of her grandmother, The Girl asks that The Woman return attention to her. Their ritual resumes in beat sixteen, but The Girl is hesitant. There are line-switched and partial iterations of the ritual without the initiating snap in beat eighteen (503, 505), and The Woman alters the ritual in the last lines of the play. The Woman continues to defend the other girl that The Girl hit while deflecting The Man's jealous inquiries. After The Girl concludes that the other girl's "tears were over what I had, not what I did," and prompted by The Man's question, The Woman reveals that the other girl, for whom reality was too little, violently killed her baby. The Girl responds, "She took my cardboard, or would have."

The Man recalls their former intimacies to The Woman, and using imagery and phrasing from the beginning of the play, urges her to remember walking in the former garden with him, to which she says, "No; I think you're mistaken. You look familiar, though" (500). Through this, The Girl articulates a set of principles but twice delays stating the fourth principle. After The Man answers her question "*How* did I make you cry?" The Woman says, "Well…I'm sorry," which prompts The Girl's statement of her fourth principle, "I'm sorry is never enough," as if she was waiting for what she knew would be said. Recalling that in the past The Woman had said "I'm sorry I made you cry" without literally seeing him cry, The Man says, "[Y]ou knew what I would do." Compare these examples of prescience inspired by other-directed attention with The Woman's response to the recorded meta-voice that announces the play's twenty beats (503), a voice that the others presumably do not hear. This highlights The Woman's ability to be outside her personal experience, distant from others even while listening to them.

The Girl tends to define reality to suit her needs and tends to isolate herself but simultaneously craves a degree of attention that The Woman will not give. The Woman chides The Girl for crying at the sight of her own blood each month, citing the regular menstruation of "every woman from the dawn of time," which The Girl counters by saying, "I am the only one." The Woman says, "*[E]very*one is the only one," simultaneously acknowledging the individual, personal perception of the common experience and chiding The Girl for denying the reality that there is a common experience. The Girl risks asking The Woman "What…what *would* interest you?…About me" (506). The Woman relates witnessing The Girl holding back tears upon the realization that The Girl's family and friends would not come to see her anymore. Against the ideal of facing stark reality, The Girl counters The Woman's assertion that The Girl sent her visitors away and wouldn't see them with "What can happen if I won't admit it?" before jumping into the fountain (509). Of The Girl's holding back tears, The Woman muses, "Well, without a soul to hear…why shouldn't she?" and laughs off The Man's "You were there." The Girl, desperate for The Woman's verbal confirmation of her existence one way or another, says, "I didn't *hear* you!" The Woman replies, "I didn't answer you" (511-2).

The Man urges The Woman to make a vulnerable admission of when and why she has cried. She lists "all the things," concluding with "I cried when *I*…died," perhaps a reference to her choice to isolate herself from even the memory of contact. To The Man's "*Reveal* yourself!" she says, "There is no revelation *in* me" (512-3). The Woman seems on the verge of a personal reflection when she says "Blood doesn't bother me much. It did once, though!" (resonant with "personal, once" from the beginning of the play, 453) before relating a story of being approached in the park by a girl who said "Do you want me to *show* you something?" (recalling "*I'll* show you something"; 454, 500). The girl had slit her wrists and "drawn her hands from pockets filled with her blood." (The park, The Woman's book, the approach of a suicidal stranger, and The Man's "Oh, God!" all recall *The Zoo Story*.) At this, The Girl brings her blood-covered hands over the edge of the fountain and says, "Like this?" The Girl is not crying at the sight of her own blood. The Man exhorts The Woman to do something but does nothing himself. The Girl taunts, "You said you could hear my pupils widen.... [Y]ou don't *listen*," to which The Woman chillingly replies, "*I* listen" (515-8). One can listen without attending to, without caring for, without helping another, perhaps even engaging only to invoke distress or harm.

Usually some insight into the circumstances of Albee's damaged children can be gleaned from the text. Here the cause of The Girl's trauma is unknown. She rejects her family (she "sent them off," 508), and therefore there is no exploration of marriage or family bonds or conflicts here. But The Woman's description of The Girl's family doesn't seem problematic. The other girl under The Woman's charge rejected her family as well by violently killing her baby. Rejecting The Man's characterization of The Girl as a butterfly, The Woman equates her to a praying mantis (457), an image recalled when The Woman describes the visit of The Girl's family, which includes a dog (508). The Man expresses admiration for The Girl with "She *is* an animal, isn't she" (460). The putative contents of the fountain—bones, egg/shell, feather—are associated with animals (468-9). The Woman recalls crying for her cats (513).

The Woman questions the reality of her past relationship with The Man throughout the play, from "*Did* I hold your hand?" (455) to "Was it *you*?" (513) The Woman asks The Man "How do you know who's what!?" (465) The Girl asks The Man "Are *you* real?" (475) Denying that the other girl cried when hit, The Girl says, "I didn't see it, so it didn't happen" (478). Questioning the reality of The Woman's speech about her grandmother's thoughts on life, The Man says, "You remember all that, every comma; and you so little" (489). The Woman chastises The Girl with "maybe conscious lies are an improvement" (491) and says that the other girl is in her care because she said "Reality is too *little* for me" (492) before killing her baby. Denying that she sent her family and friends away, The Girl says, "What can happen if I won't admit it?" (509). The Woman's speech about what she's cried over is a litany of harsh realities (513). "Who am I?" is often asked by Albee's characters in their quest to articulate an identity. Here The Woman uses that question to deflect introspection (480). When lines are switched in the ritual exchange, The Girl exclaims, "Don't twist me! I'm…me!" (503) Questioning identity often leads to questioning existence in Albee's work. Here, The Girl says, "[I]t either *is* there, or is not…as am *I*" (510), and pleads for confirmation of whether or not she exists (512).

As usual, there is much attention to language. The Man corrects "circular" to "semicircular" in his first speech (453). The Woman makes a pun about giving The Girl "something she can chew on" just after referring to her as a praying mantis (459, 457). There is hairsplitting over "egg" versus "egg shell" (469-70), a choice to add a suffix (openhanded, 474), and this exhortation that implies interpretation must accompany text: "By look around, I didn't mean to look around. I meant…look *around*" (477). The Woman consciously uses "who" instead of "whom" (484) and chuckles over the oddity of "you never *know*. You know?" just before saying "it was a generation wouldn't let you know, you know?" (486, 487) All the characters effect emotional distance from one another with an occasional "*actor's reading*" or "*playacting version*" of their lines (455, 505). There is resonance with *Hedda Gabler* in The Woman's "Done beautifully" (517). The Woman's emphasis on the possibility of glass in the fountain and her evocative story of the bleeding girl may imply that The Woman is urging The Girl to an elegant suicide as Hedda does Lovborg.

The repetitive nature of the play is established in the first beat as The Man says that his environment is "Very much as" promised, stated, announced, imagined, and suggested (453-4). In addition to the exchange between The Woman and The Girl, The Woman and The Man exchange "You're not nice" or "Be nice" and "Who's nice?" throughout the play (first on 472, last on 514). Beat eighteen recalls some of the imagery and phrasing of beat one. Albee gives The Woman captivating speeches about her grandparents (487-9), what she cried over (513), and the girl in the park (515-6).

All three characters have abstracted names and are placed in an open environment with "*sky behind*" (452) as in the early plays. The Voice is "*recorded*" (452), a condition not specified for Voice in *Box* (cf. 263). *Listening* was originally commissioned for radio (8): note The Man's explicit description of the fountain and environs for the listener in the first beat and his announcement of The Girl's leap into the fountain (453, 510). Note also the emphasis on the aural, both concrete and abstract: the sound of footfall on patio stone (453-4) and the sound an idea makes (464). Although The Voice announces twenty beats, the play flows without division and builds to a climactic event; but the play is more cyclical than climactic, its central theme being that attention can be impersonal. Albee's next play, a vaudeville composed to be performed before this chamber play (8), features a comparable number of beats that will be divided into episodes separated by blackouts.

COUNTING THE WAYS

III. The Veneer We Call Civilization

Counting the Ways

Counting the Ways explores how civilized thought puts us at a distance from the visceral reality of animal instinct, of love and pain.

I. Love Means Sex? (*2CP* 523-528)

The play begins with He and She reading. Rather than simply taking it for granted, She desires to know the answer to the question "Do you *love* me?" and fears the answer she'll be offered. He, taking it for granted, answers, "Of course." In Scene Two, when She asks the question again at the end of a grocery list, He hungrily answers, "Of course!" equating love with sensory pleasure rather than with an abstract idea. But in Scene Three, She describes He's problems attaining sexual arousal and the effect is has on her ("There are deserts"; cf. Himself in *The Man Who Had Three Arms*: "[T]here are oases," *3CP*

148). She predicts that his ability will one day cease and proclaims that going on "knowing all that" is called love. As her grandmother (she thinks it was) said, "*[L]ove* doesn't die; we pass *through* it." Love in the morning and love in the afternoon are equated with sex, but love at night is equated with the complex tensions of adult relationships, with reality, and therefore "has to be love."

II. Roses (*2CP* 529-539)

He, too, desires to know if She loves him and fears the answer that She might offer. Discovering that He has been playing "She loves me. She loves me not" with the petals of a rose, She says, "Why didn't you just *ask* me?" Of his eating the petals that were left She says, "You just didn't want to know!...Ask *me! I'll* tell you!" to which He says, exiting, "I'll get another one," which prompts her to pick up the petals and play the game in reverse. He returns with two roses. She says of her new rose and his new rose, "[T]hey should be together; one of us should have them both." His resistant "What will you do, make an arrangement?" drives her off. His reluctant offer of his rose brings her back and prompts her remembrance of the shy boy who misunderstood that he wasn't her prom date and offered her a second gardenia. She thinks about him "from time to time, during love." Of the roses, she says, making another reference to love losing (sexual) potency over time, "These will wilt!" He has been looking for his shirts during She's remembrance, proclaiming, "Thousands have lived without love, but none without shirts," (or "without Crème Brulee") with apologies to Auden. He proposes a philosophy of distance, asserting that pain is a misunderstanding of loss and that life is mostly "going on *without* something." She asserts that the roses (the ones she said should be together) "should be on the table...between our [newly separate] beds!"

III. The Veneer We Call Civilization (*2CP* 539-554)

He insists upon, and She resists, discussion of why there are now two beds. Continuing the idea of the loss of love's potential over time, She says, "[I]t's been coming," and that if they're lucky it won't devolve into "separate rooms." Acknowledging that all of us might one day find or have found ourselves in He and She's situation, Albee breaks with civilized theatrical convention by having the actors break character to address the audience as themselves in an Entre Scene. Resuming character, She relates "a test of protocol" concerning two dying men ("well, we all are, but these two are *closer* to it") that she believes her sister has given to her in order to "collapse" civilization: "the veneer we call civilization" that coats our animal nature being as tenuous under heat as the "caramel that coats the Crème Brulee." Scenes Sixteen and Eighteen provide a comical look at civilizing distance as He and She work to remember how many children they have. In Scene Seventeen, He, resonant with his philosophy of distance earlier, ponders the concept of imaginative grief. As the play ends, She asks He if he loves her after announcing that there really is no Crème Brulee, offering Raspberry Fool instead, but then she discovers there aren't any raspberries either. She ends the play as she began, asking He, "[H]ow do you *know* you love me?" He, avoiding a considered response, assures She that he does love her, but when He then asks She, "Do *you* love *me*?" the play ends with She's answer: "I don't *know*....I *think* I do."

The essence of the play is found in He's rumination just before discovering that He and She now sleep in separate beds: "If you can get *away*, if you can *watch* your emotions, you know that pain is a misunderstanding: it's really *loss*; *loss* is what it's *really* about" (cf. Jerry: "what is gained is loss," *1CP* 31). "Most of it's slow and after the fact and has to do with going on *without* something, something we thought was necessary—essential—but then discovered it merely made all the difference: one *could* go on if one really *wanted* to" (*2CP* 538). This echoes "I can't go on, I'll go on" from the end of Samuel Beckett's novel *The Unnamable*, which signature Beckett phrase Albee references explicitly in *Finding the Sun* (*3CP* 246). He's philosophy resonates with placing the veneer we call civilization over our animal natures. He admits that his "animal instinct" to protect She might be eradicated with just "a split-second of civilized thought" (*2CP* 553). Civilized thought is at odds with facing the reality of our fears about loss and death, especially the loss and death of our love. Even in a vaudeville, Albee deftly explores the complexities of the marriage bond.

Linguistically, She notes He's move "into the historical present," "an odd tense" (540-1). She wonders whether "close-knit" family should be amended to "closely knitted?" (545) He verbally admires She's "phrasing" (553). Both He and She acknowledge the audience. Two characters acknowledging the audience has only happened here and in *Mao*, but multiple characters acknowledging the audience is about to become a regular feature of Albee's plays. This play contains the only instance of actors breaking character to speak to the audience as themselves and the only specified use of the fly space or signs in an Albee play. No playwrights are referenced, but there is an indirect reference to Poe (525) and direct references to Auden (537-8, 548).

Albee continues to use stage directions to prompt conversation with the artists who will bring his work to the stage: a combination of freedom and stricture and some confusion. He begins his description of

THE SCENE with "*I see*" (implying that you might see it differently) and ends it with "*No clutter, though!*" (520) He defers a question of timing to "*the discretion of the director*" (532). He did not take the opportunity in 2005 to broaden his narrow suggestion about how the actress might talk about herself in the Entre Scene—"*kids, husband, etc.*" (544). He asks that *THE SIGNS* be "*Exactly as described*" and gives options for their appearance (520; cf. Avant Scene, 522). For the Entre Scene, he implies that the sign may be replaced with a voice (544), and for the end of the play, he calls for a voice to announce *THE END*; there is no mention of a sign (554). Perhaps the distant, unseen voice replacing the visible signs is meant to reflect a growing distance in He and She's relationship. The voice segues nicely into *Listening* as well.

The repetition of the grocery list (524, 538, 549) and the similarity of the opening and closing beats give the play a hint of ritual, and Albee gives us several of his usual finely crafted monologues in this play. Albee places his characters (a pair with abstracted names) in an open, explicitly sparse environment. This is the only play in which Albee presents a series of vaudevillian vignettes divided by blackouts (the signs and actors breaking character providing further touches of a Brechtian distancing effect), but although the play is structured episodically, it is also centered on the idea that the veneer we call civilization dampens our animal instincts.

THE LADY FROM DUBUQUE

The Lady from Dubuque

The Lady from Dubuque exposes "the rights we pretend we give ourselves" (*2CP* 657) and suggests that, given the volatility of values such as "liberty, dignity, possession," knowing who we are is the only value that matters (662).

I. Your Nice, Average, Desperate Evening (*2CP* 561-608)

The play opens with trivial dialogue spoken by a trio of couples playing a trivial game of twenty questions (in which participants guess the assumed rather than the actual identities of others). The couples manifest a range of potential power relationships—male-dominant, relative equality, female-dominant—through what is putatively an evening of fun among friends, but as Fred says, "[T]hese social events are wearing on a man." Between the couples and in the individual relationships, the exchanges devolve into meanness born of personal insecurities. To Sam's

"Why do we have them over, Jo?" Jo says, "[B]ecause we need a surface to bounce it all off of…and because we probably do love them in spite of everything" (591). Jo's brutal honesty with her friend Lucinda is "breaking [Lucinda's] heart," so Lucinda's husband Edgar urges Jo to go to Lucinda, who is crying on Jo's lawn, and to help Lucinda "because she's in pain down there, too, and she didn't cause yours" (594).

The contradiction between our desires and what other people offer us is palpable when our friends and family hurt us, when they want to wish away reality, and when we want opposing things simultaneously. Of the impending loss of Jo, his dying wife, Sam says, "The thing we must do about loss is, hold on to the object we're losing. There's time later for… ourselves." Jo counters Sam's assertion that he shares her pain with stark reality: "No, you don't, and I'm glad. Yours is almost all in your head—in your mind, I mean—and mine isn't." And to his resistance to her description of pain, she says, "Don't cover up like that!…if you can't take it now, what will you be like when I *need* you?" Of dying, she says, "[T]he day comes you realize you've known but haven't admitted it." Sam says, "You tell me to ignore you when you get like this, and then you yell at me." To Jo's "I've got to have it both ways. Don't pay any attention. Pay attention? Please?" Sam says, defeated, "Whatever you want" (600-5). The commitment to stark reality is underlined by Albee having all the characters in this play address or appeal to the audience, so there is no pretense from any character that the audience is not there. This also creates a meta-awareness which is heightened when two mysterious characters enter not through doors, but *"from without the set"* to close the play's first act.

II. Peace Descends (*2CP* 609-669)

In contrast to the triviality of the play's opening sequence of Twenty Questions and repetitions of "Who am I?" Sam, on the following morning, grows increasingly desperate and afraid with each repetition of "Who are you?" to Elizabeth. References to Marx and Engels (610, 613; cf. 566) underline the contrast to the opening sequence. Determining the identity of the strangers is imperative, not trivial. Albee's concern with identity in this play encompasses attention to race, gender, stereotypes, and insensitivity. The title of the play was inspired by a stereotypical remark (cf. Gussow 310); Sam's nickname, "Sambo," recalls a racist stereotype; Elizabeth's companion, Oscar, jokingly uses Hitler's phrase "final solution" (649). Oscar appears to be calling attention to the white characters' discomfort with racial difference, malicious in Fred's case (631). Oscar's use of racist epithets to refer to himself (619, 643) and emulation of racist stereotypes (621, 663) might be in service to creating white discomfort, but Oscar's words and phrases are at best awkward and at worst disrespectful coming from a white author whose reference to "*street blacks*" in his stage directions (624, 636) could be perceived as condescension. Albee could have revisited that 1980 phrase; Elizabeth's assertion that a "*real* Bush will come along one day, if the Russians don't" (657)—prescient given the rise of Trump and his ties to Russia—appears in the 2005 collection. Oscar and Elizabeth are equals of higher status than the other characters, but note that Elizabeth lightly dismisses Oscar when he playfully questions her metaphorical use of "dogs" in reference to him (624). Albee's approach to this social arrangement, a black man surrounded by white people, evolves with Man 2 in *Fragments* (cf. *3CP* 437). Edgar espouses a traditional philosophy of male-dominated marriage (2CP 596, 598), although Fred believes that Edgar's wife, Lucinda, is in control of Edgar's behavior (575). Fred disparages "sex changes" (565), is mockingly prissy (650), and is deemed by Jo to be a "fag baiter" (592) and "unworthy of human solicitude" (646). Fred's violent tendencies are seen when he punches Sam (658) and sweeps the coffee service to the floor (659, perhaps a hint of Stevie's more rampant destruction of objects forthcoming in *The Goat*). Although Carol is powerful enough to counter Fred's tantrum with a threat of her own, she still is compelled to close down and make the bad choice of marrying him. The last of several flippant reasons she gives for marrying him perhaps derives from lingering fears born of generations of power bias in gender relationships: "I'm not twenty-two anymore, and I'm scared" (661). The contradiction between our desires and what other people offer us is also palpable when our loneliness and fear drive us to make bad choices.

Elizabeth and Oscar have otherworldly awareness and abilities. Although Elizabeth claims to be Jo's mother, she and Oscar are actually angels of death, like the Young Man from *The Sandbox* (Elizabeth's eloquent dream about dying occurs "on a beach at sunset," 666-7). Jo, in pain and near death, accepts Elizabeth's comfort and does not resist Elizabeth's claim to be Jo's mother as Sam does, given that it runs counter to what Jo has told him. Aware of events in the first act she was not there to hear, Elizabeth, in repeating it, elevates Jo's trivial phrase from the night before: "The man has asked for silence; give it to him" (637; cf. 561, 562). Oscar is able to make Sam unconscious by touching him (640) and near the end of the play adorns Sam's nightshirt to take Jo upstairs as Sam did to close the first act, although Jo will not come downstairs again after ascending with Oscar. Elizabeth's meta-perspective extends to a discussion of the reality of needs and rights and dignity and dying and identity. Sam's need for Jo is keeping Jo from what she needs, and therefore Elizabeth arrives to force Sam to face the stark reality of Jo's dying: "He wasn't happy with the way things are. He wanted everything back the way it never was" (649). Lucinda's accusation of Sam—"you don't love anyone" (653)—recalls what The Woman says when she loses her spouse at the end of *All Over* (365). Elizabeth speaks to Sam about how rights and dignity are swept away by death (657; cf. the dead "who are nothing," 652) and about how there's only one value that matters: "Who am I?" To Sam's "I don't know who I am" (cf. Jo in the game that opens the play: "he doesn't know who he is," 562) Elizabeth says, "Then how can you possibly know who I am?" (662). To Sam's "Who are you? Really?" Elizabeth gives an answer that ties her identity to her account of her learned experience: "I'm the lady from Dubuque" (669, cf. 662).

Elizabeth learned about the value of identity "with all the pigs and chickens and the endless sameness everywhere you looked" (662) and about the irrelevance of dignity from "a dog named Dignity…or, that was her name when I got her; I changed it; I called her Jane. She's dead" (657). Sam ties his identity to his relationship with his wife. Of Jo's choice to die, he says, "[Y]ou've locked me out. I…I don't exist" (665). Resonant with Charlie's reaction to Leslie and Sarah in *Seascape*, Sam questions the reality of Elizabeth and Oscar: "You aren't really here, are you?" and "*I* exist; *you* don't" (624). Elizabeth speaks of "the rights we pretend we give ourselves" (657). Oscar questions Carol's assertion that "Things are either true or they're not" (650), and to Elizabeth's "Everything is true" Oscar counters, "Therefore, nothing is true," to which Elizabeth counters, "Therefore, everything is true" (667-8). David Marcia asserts that the couples would rather remain closed down than face the reality of Jo's dying:

> Jo's suffering throws her surrounding social sphere into an unwelcome chaos, rubbing the noses of all in an unmitigated reality they simply will not confront. This is clearly an ethical and moral failing, the willful inability to do anything but possess the others they recognize themselves in and

through. These characters fail to acknowledge another's suffering and their own precarious existence not because it is beyond them to do so but because it would disrupt their highly cultivated comfortable numbness. (Marcia 66)

In addition to the sharp wit of the characters' meanness to each other, Jo wittily paraphrases her doctor: "[Y]ou're winding down, so…wind it up" (603). Oscar characterizes one of his baby-talk words as an adjective (612) and questions his own usage of "spillage" (654). Martha, Claire, and The Woman from *Listening* have also indulged in the distortions of baby talk, and Albee also distorts deep and dreamless to "dreap and deemless" here (641). In this play in which all of his characters address the audience, often seeking the audience's complicity rather than simply narrating facts and opinions, Albee provides a meticulous note about the nature of these exchanges (559). Regarding theatrical allusions, Kaufman and Hart and Gilbert and Sullivan are referenced in the Twenty Questions game (566), and Sarah Bernhardt is evoked for a stage direction (593). The repetitions of the questions and phrases at the beginning of the acts and Jo's ascension at the ends of the acts provide a hint of ritual, and there are powerful speeches in Edgar's defense of Lucinda (594) and Elizabeth's evocation of dying (611, 666-7). This climactic play features four paired couples in a closed (but uncluttered) environment; the next play will be episodic and open with no paired characters. Multiple characters will acknowledge the audience, though.

LOLITA

Pages   Outline
(*3CP*)

I.   Some Sudden, Impetuous Cascade of Events

II. Love; Loss; Revenge

Lolita

There is usually a direct correlation between desire and failure to face stark reality. A Certain Gentleman (ACG)—the character is an amalgam of Albee and Nabokov, whose novel Albee adapts here—describes Humbert's desire for Lolita as "an unreasonable passion" and "[o]bsession; delusion; enthrallment" (*3CP* 75, 83). ACG counters Humbert's assertion that Humbert loves Lolita with "But does *she* love *you*?" to which Humbert says, "I don't want to know" (74).

I. Some Sudden, Impetuous Cascade of Events (*3CP* 11-69)

ACG and Humbert are even more inclusive of the audience than were the characters in *The Lady from Dubuque* (this trend continues in *The Man Who Had Three Arms, The Play About the Baby*, and *Occupant*). Unlike the novel, which is solely from Humbert's perspective, the play allows us to see the contrast between Humbert's idealization of Lolita as nymphet (22) and Lolita's natural, grounded behavior throughout the play. To counter the nymphet claim, ACG describes Lolita as "an ordinary little girl" (32). After introducing Humbert, ACG stays onstage to challenge him, a source of tension and humor who gives us a more objective view of Humbert's subjective philosophies, reveries, and obsessions. ACG questions Humbert's assertion that there can be "perfectly rational relationships" between people and animals (15), which foreshadows *The Goat*. Speaking of *The Goat* in 2005, Albee said, "I wanted people to go to that play, and imagine themselves in the situation, and really think hard about how they would respond if it was happening to them" (*SMM* 284). Here, ACG, as he pulls a curtain in front of the pre-coital Humbert and Lolita, says, "You can imagine it," and suggests that we may have imagined it or dreamed it and blanked it from our minds (*3CP* 65). Humbert wonders if anyone in the audience sees Lolita as he does: "Is there a pedophile in the house?" (32) Humbert also asserts that in some cultures "grown men are wed to girls of ten, and no one thinks twice, but I am a criminal" (22). To ACG's charge that Humbert's "criminal mind" can't fathom Charlotte's sincerity, Humbert counters, "*I* am sincere" (41-2).

Albee has a rare lapse of sincerity in a few of the character-audience exchanges in this play. Both ACG and Humbert say "Good evening" (11, 13) as they enter, and Albee notes "*Or afternoon*" in the stage directions, which is an example of the usual care Albee takes to be true to the present moment onstage. But upon his entrance ACG reacts as if some of the audience members have applauded, which is not a guaranteed occurrence. Normally, Albee would plan for alternate responses in his stage directions. In *The Play About the Baby*, when Man asks a particular audience member a question, Albee instructs, "*If no answer, go on; if there's an answer, improvise briefly*" (466), and later, "*If anyone answers, handle it*" (507). When Albee needs guaranteed applause to open *Occupant*, he calls for "*canned applause—whistles, etc.*" (626), which works because Nevelson is still in her "cage," and Man and Nevelson's honest exchanges with the audience are yet to be established. Here, there is no call for canned applause to start the play, but near the end of the first act, to ridicule Humbert for thinking Lolita is a virgin, Albee has the theatre fill "*with many laughters, mocking cries, hoots*" (61); not necessarily canned, but also not attributed to characters in the play and only heard by Humbert. While this symbolizes Humbert's paranoia, unattributed sounds heard only by Humbert do not continue to accompany Humbert's growing paranoia as the play progresses, so in this case the single use of the sound effect seems forced. Likely, Albee imposes the sounds to justify Humbert's initiation of the sequence of Nabokov-Albee puns with "Laughter in the Dark" (62). Also, Albee has ACG deliver a shallow speech to "*someone particular in the audience*" (11), implying that ACG attended a party with the audience member, an odd imposition of circumstance which rings false. Again, Albee could have revisited this text for the 2005 edition, which includes several typographical and copy-editing problems, including an instance of character speeches out of order (104).

Albee continues to explore racist attitudes and other fears as he has in *The Death of Bessie Smith*, *Everything in the Garden*, and *The Lady from Dubuque*. Charlotte's racism (26-7) is inherited by Lolita (76), who also characterizes herself as Humbert's "WHITE SLAVE" (72) rather than as his sex slave. Quilty calls Humbert an "escapee from the ovens" (125, cf. 127), and Charlotte, frustrated by Humbert's inattention, asks if he's "a fairy" (40). Charlotte, "a liberated woman" who thinks "Sex is healthy" and whose first husband was not ready for her (42), has perhaps also influenced Lolita's openness to sexual experience. While

Lolita does object to Humbert's sexual coercion and eccentricities, she is even more upset by his possessiveness. Humbert's pathological self-interest is seen at the end of the first act when he is unable to comfort a grieving Lolita without coaxing her to fellate him. This is the most disturbing imagery of parental betrayal and abuse since Young Man's twin's dismemberment by his parents in *The American Dream*. Lolita's loss of innocence and her practical nature also resonate with Young Man, an avatar of whom will appear in the second act.

II. Love; Loss; Revenge (*3CP* 70-135)

ACG tries to coax Humbert into admitting his denial of reality—"[you think that] if you keep her with you, fleeing across this county, suspending time, she will stay as she is. But will she?"—but Humbert resists ACG's tactics. To ACG's "But does *she* love *you*?" Humbert coldly replies, "I don't want to know," which resonates with She's response to He's eating the rose petals in *Counting the Ways*: "You just didn't want to know!" (*2CP* 531) To signify Quilty's chasing of Humbert and Lolita across the country, Albee has Quilty impersonate characters they encounter: a female psychologist and the Groucho Marx-inspired doctor who facilitates Lolita's escape. Humbert retraces his path back through all the motels he has shared with Lolita to look for proof of Quilty's presence, as obsessed with revenging himself against Quilty as he is with losing Lolita. Humbert makes this journey with a new companion, Rita, and the pair have apparently picked up a Young Man, who wakes in their room. Like the Young Man of *The American Dream*, this Young Man doesn't know who he is and is the object of sexual attention (3CP 101) from a parental figure (Rita, 104), establishing a parallel between the damaged Young Man of *The American Dream* and Lolita.

Humbert, indifferent and doubting his existence after she is taken from him, is granted a reunion with Lolita and her new husband by ACG. Humbert says, through clenched teeth, "I'm so glad you're happy," to which Lolita, who has no problem facing stark reality, replies, "I didn't say I was happy; I'm content." When Humbert asks "You never loved me?" she says, "No; I guess not.... [T]hat's the way it was; that's the way it is....You always told me to be honest" (115, 117). Unlike in the novel, Albee doesn't have Humbert articulate his realization that he has deprived Lolita of her childhood, but Albee does have Humbert shoot Quilty multiple times before Quilty succumbs to death. This must be handled carefully onstage to keep from becoming unintentionally comic, but even if that devolution were to occur, the performance would still be rescued by Albee's masterful ability to craft ritual sadness out of simple dialogue. Albee brings the play to a poignant end by having ACG inform Humbert of his impending death as well as the death of Lolita in childbirth and, an hour or so later, of her child, given by Lolita's husband the name of Lolita's father, for whom Humbert was mistaken. This justifies ACG's claim to the Young Man: "[I]t's a story of ghosts" (100).

Although Humbert becomes a husband and stepfather in the course of the play, he is far too self-absorbed for there to be any of Albee's usual exploration of familial bonds and conflicts here. As in *The Lady from Dubuque*, self-concern and need are detrimental to the articulation of identity. At Charlotte's visitation, Humbert says, "I am not myself" and "Though, if I am not myself, who am I?" (47) A disguised Quilty says to Humbert, "[W]e all create our own identity, do we not?" and "[Y]ou don't know who you are, do you?" (80-1) The Young Man asks, "[W]ho am *I*?" (97) because he has no memory of himself. However,

Lolita, the most resilient of Albee's damaged children, expresses her sense of self quite clearly to Humbert: "You don't love me; all you love is my body!" (71) and "Don't call me your pet; what do you think I am—a dog or something?" (33) ACG, justifying his claim that we have imagined unsettling sexual scenarios in "dreams you deny to your waking mind," asserts, "We are animals, remember, not far from the baboon, and circumspection is often confused with civilization" (65). Motels "give a sense of unreality" (57), and Humbert uses them to give himself the illusion of suspending time and the fact that Lolita will grow older (67, 74). Humbert decides to believe he has given Lolita a hickey he can't remember because "there's no alternative…none I can accept" (78). In contrast, Lolita always asserts stark reality: "The word is incest, Dad" (63). Again, as in *The Lady from Dubuque*, the loss of love is tied to loss of existence (104, 119, 133), and like Sam, Humbert, holding his ears when ACG presents him with the reality of Lolita's voice, is admonished to "Take your cowardly hands away!" (105) Faced with the reality of Lolita's life without him, Humbert says goodbye to her as "*darkness engulfs*" her onstage (120). Recalling this moment, ACG says, "You saw her vanish" (133).

ACG and Humbert's frequent interaction with the audience (and acknowledgement of the audience by Lolita, Charlotte, Annabel, and Rita) help establish the meta-awareness of *Lolita* as a story being manipulated by those presenting it. Both ACG and Quilty make comments about Humbert's writing style (36, 130), and when Charlotte discovers Humbert's diary (thanks to ACG), Humbert defends it as "notes for a book" (44): in a sense we are watching an adaptation of the book that came from that diary. Theatrical conventions remind us that we are watching the creation and manipulation of a story. Annabel objects, "I'm dead," when called back to the stage by Humbert (21).

The text calls attention to the fact that Louise and Quilty are playing other characters as well (the speech headings are attributed to Louise and Quilty in these cases), and in the nebulous transition of scene from hotel to hospital, Louise is addressed as all three of her characters in successive farewells. Lolita resists the blackout that takes her out of the play (120). Albee masterfully uses the intermission, a brief suspension of the narrative, to reflect Humbert's wish to suspend time. Albee, always looking for ways to avoid false contrivance (except for a moment or two in this play), will have his characters make honest, direct reference to intermissions just before the break in four (and just after the break in one) of his later plays.

ACG's lamentation of "art as commodity" (11) and assessment of Quilty as a "*Terrible* writer; makes a fortune! Works in film now" (30) resonate with the unfavorable characterization of musical theatre in *Fragments* (406), a play that makes reference to Albee in the text (396-402). *Lolita*, a play with three author characters, features allusions to the works of Albee and Nabokov (62, 64, 97), allusions to Poe (17) and Yeats (105, 122), and references to Poe and Eliot (129) and the Absurdists (66). Humbert appropriates Iago's revenge-plot language—"But he that filches from me my good name"—substituting "my nymphet" (96) for "my name," an indication of the extremity of Humbert's possessiveness of Lolita. In addition to the playfully gratuitous use of Albee and Nabokov titles (62) and substitution of Coverlet for Quilty (89), there are the following jovial juxtapositions: "abominable—abdominal" (62), "menage" and "manage" (94), and "*Fondly, fondling*" (102). The perversely impish witticisms and figures of speech (60, 103) continue even into the play's poignant ending with ACG's "Come and go" (134). There are also instances of Albee's linguistic eloquence, as in ACG's paean to mutability (88).

ACG and Humbert's frequent exchanges with the audience will inspire characters in about half of Albee's remaining plays, including Himself's long presentation in the next play, which marks a return to abstracted names for all its characters. Although many of Albee's remaining plays feature personal stories that span a lifetime, these stories are told to the audience and to other characters rather than enacted, and therefore Albee's next nine plays will not require a change of scenery.

THE MAN WHO HAD THREE ARMS

Pages   Outline
(*3CP*)

I. This Is My Life

II. I Have Always Been *You*

The Man Who Had
Three Arms

The Man Who Had Three Arms reveals how reality and personal identity are shaped in relation to others and have little context, meaning, or worth without others and reveals how the gap between what we desire and what we are offered from others is despairingly wide. Himself experiences both the "acceptable pattern" of "individuality within conformity" (*3CP* 177) and the intensified "sense of self" that accompanies the potential to affect "public perception" (187).

I. This Is My Life (*3CP* 140-165)

Himself, the titular character of *The Man Who Had Three Arms*, is the guest of an organization that has hosted "men and women whose accomplishments have wreaked their order on our havoc...and identified our reality by creating it for us" (145). Man introduces Woman (as Madame President), who then makes announcements and begins introducing Himself, who enters before his name is spoken. The lack of a specific name gives Himself a universality that bolsters his claim at the end of the play that "I have always been *you*" (193).

There is more direct address to the audience in this play than in any other Albee play, with the possible exceptions of *The Play About the Baby* and *Occupant*, and Albee takes great care to call for realistic interaction with the audience in his text and stage directions. After Man's "tonight," Albee notes "*or 'this afternoon' as the situation demands*" (141; cf. 143, 146, 147, 150). Himself is "however old the actor playing HIMSELF is" (155; cf. instructions based on the actor's race, 156). And Himself will call for the second act to begin "fifteen minutes from whatever time it is" (165). When Himself singles out audience members (145-6), he asks them questions they can answer truthfully, the only imposition being the pretense that they are attending his lecture. Himself directs his ire at a journalist somewhere in the audience; but since Himself does not single out a particular audience member for this, the illusion that the journalist is out there is better served than when ACG pretends he knows a particular audience member from a party in *Lolita* (11). In contrast to this meticulous awareness of audience interaction, as in *Lolita* there is an expectation of applause with no qualifying stage direction in case there isn't (142). There is also an expectation of laughter without a qualifying stage direction in the first act (147), but then a call for canned laughter in the second act (178). Also, presumably each production of the play is meant to occur in the present, so "Seven times a year for thirty-three years we have gathered here" (141) would have to be replaced with "For years we have gathered here" or references to Einstein and Hoover removed if the play is not to stay locked in the time of its 1983 premiere.

At pre-talk meals on the lecture circuit, back when Himself had three arms, "They would look at me, these people; I would look at *them*. I would unfocus my eyes, finally, stare off into the middle distance—humiliated by my specialness. I hadn't split the atom; I hadn't written fifteen string quartets, or saved the country from itself. I'd grown a fucking third arm! Where's the talent in that?" (148) Himself's story is delayed a bit when pornographic slides are discovered in place of his opening images, but the mistake underscores Himself's lament that the audience wants "the climax at the beginning." He appeals to the audience for respect: "I am not a freak. I am an average gentleman." During Himself's anecdote of the priest, for his presentation of "HOW IT ALL BEGAN," and for the remainder of his story in the second act, Man and Woman "*momentarily assume*" roles as prompted by Himself's narrative.

Himself's stare "into the middle distance" recalls the dying man's "faint shift from total engagement" (*2CP* 311) in *All Over*. The themes of *Tiny Alice* make their way into Himself's excoriation of the priest (*3CP* 151). Himself's Man A, who "keeps his eyes closed so as not to see too much," resonates with Albee's themes of closing down and lost potential. Man C's "eyes burned out by the glory" (151-2) resonates with Kermit, who "can't bear the splendor" of the Girards' chateau in *Malcolm* (*1CP* 586). Also, Himself says that his wife "couldn't take the blinding light" of his fame (*3CP* 187). Himself's characterization of God's test—"I love you. Do you love me?" (153)—recalls *Counting the Ways*. Albee's plays continue to reflect the ugly currents of tolerated racial and gender discrimination and stereotyping that mar our interaction with each other. Himself, who Albee notes in his stage directions can be played by a black actor (156), characterizes the priest and his parents ("Forgive them; they were good people") as having racist tendencies (154, 159). Himself uses "lesbo" disparagingly (163) but sympathizes or at least recognizes the potential loneliness of a "gay" with a "*normal face*" in a "*town like any other town*" (155-6).

Also, although "set flame to the faggots" is surely a reference to wood (146), Albee is also surely calling attention to the dual meanings of a word. Himself propagates the stereotype of easy versus marriageable girls (160). Characterizing the press as opinionated and unfair, Himself shouts "Cunt!" at the audience (a decorum breach on the order of pointing a gun at them), which putatively includes (one of) the female journalist(s) who hounds him. Himself is conscious of how that word offends Woman but uses it twice more anyway (163-5). Just before insisting upon an intermission, Himself, who is somewhat abrasive to others, again insists upon respect for himself: "If you come upon me, my back to you, my shoulders shaking with my sobbing, please leave me be; don't…touch me, comfortingly, gently, on the golden spot; don't offer solace. Just…leave me be and let me sob it out" (165).

II. I Have Always Been *You* (*3CP* 166-194)

The second act commences with Himself hounding the audience into their seats and taunting his hosts. Albee takes care to provide instructions for varying performance conditions in his stage directions (167, 169), but then has Himself state that he spoke with a "ten-year-old boy, hideous glasses, likewise suit, teeth like a rabbit" (168) during the intermission. Unlike the more general description of the journalist, these are characteristics we could spot (or, more likely, not spot) as we exit productions given in smaller theatres where we might notice everyone who leaves. We could ask "Why didn't we see Himself at intermission?" too. When Himself says of his exchange with the journalist at intermission "I crashed my hand into her crotch like a goosing twelve-year-old," Man and Woman's impulse is to deny that such an offense would occur. Himself reiterates, "I was physically abusive to a lady" (168). Albee's comment on the license taken by the famous and on our willful denial of stark reality is still applicable. Almost half of the people who voted in the 2016 United States presidential election denied (or dismissed) the reality of a presidential candidate's boast: "Grab 'em by the pussy. You can do anything." The candidate, who went on to win the election, did not admit that his behavior was physically abusive, but rather enabled the public's denial, characterizing his admission of assault as harmless locker-room talk, although the candidate was older than twelve when the admission was recorded. Himself's preference for traditional gender roles leads him to sarcasm in response to strong women, saying "You've got balls" to the journalist and "Yes, Sir" at Woman's insistence that he "Get on with it!" (168-9) In contrast to Himself's accusation of "Abandoner!" we hear, through Woman, his wife's excoriation of Himself's failure of character and her revelation of sexual assaults by the third arm while Himself slept (186).

One of the most telling statements Himself makes is that he finds it "hard sometimes to distinguish between my self-disgust and my disgust with others" but that he "can tell self-pity from the Christlike a mile away—well, a hundred yards" (169). Before the growth of the third arm Himself had "settled into an acceptable pattern—individuality within conformity" (177). He says that he did not want what happened and that his career was destroyed by it (183), but he also relishes "the awareness of *self* that comes as revelation, the knowledge that one *is* larger than life, at least larger than others; the fact that one can change whole areas of public perception, help alter the course of history" (187). Upon the loss of the arm, Himself realized that he had not "carried too many friends along with me to the heights of my celebrity" and that "for a year and a half I sat, staring off into the middle distance" (192), the middle distance being Albee's representation of the unbridgeable gap between desire and offer, between self and other. His celebrity reduced, Himself pleads with his audience, hatefully, "I'm no different from you; I'm just like everyone you know; you love *them*; you love *me*. Stop treating me like a freak! I am *not* a freak! I am *you*! I have always *been* you! I am YOU!!! Stop looking at me!! Like that!!" (193) When it seems the arm is returning, his earnest pleading changes to "It's coming back, you fuckers," but Himself is stunned by the revelation that what Man and Woman see growing out of his back are toes.

Our dependence on others to give our reality context is comically represented by Man's musing after he says Woman needs no introduction: "Why am I here at all? Is all illusion? Do I exist?" (142) Woman says their organization invites speakers who have "identified our reality by creating it for us" (145). Himself experiences changes in his sense of self based on the nature of the attention he receives from and his influence over others. Also, without the arm, he muses "does one miss oneself" (147), but he also sees the arm as separate: in the early stages of discovery, he says "I noticed I—it!—was scratching away" (181). Woman as Himself's wife says, "Tell them how you'd go to sleep and *it* wouldn't" (186). While family bonds and conflicts are not the focus of this play, it is clear the conflict of Himself's reaction to fame sundered family bonds. One animal image of "a large pig" stands out given that it was in reference to a picture in a locket next to a picture of a zoologist under consideration for guest speaker (143), another seed of an idea that comes to flower in *The Goat*.

In addition to puns about hands, attention is also paid to linguistic syntax and meanings: "a grand march of minds across the...something of our something" (141); "Andean crevasse...which I take to be a crevasse in the Andes" (143); "wreaked their order on our havoc," which prompts Man's admiration (145); dual meanings of "committed" and "small" (147) and "foot" (189); "Is it cellophane any longer? I wonder" (152); "had a baby" ("not literally bouncing") identified as a statement of the obvious (156); "that is not precisely what I said" (157); "You can't go home again, they tell you, by which they mean you cannot become yourself as a child again" (159); and "they write with spite and polish" (163). And these two witticisms are as fine as anything in the Albee canon: "the sort of sofa gives one second thoughts about the West" (170) and "a lemonish chiffon of the density of flown hope" (148).

Albee's stage directions not only anticipate a variety of audience responses to character prompts, they also continue to acknowledge variations in design and acting choices: *"If there is no curtain"* (140) and *"Has SHE risen? I'm not sure"* (151). There are references to novelists Melville (151), Nabokov (158; and *"laughter in the dark,"* 187), and Agee (159); playwrights Coward (173) and Miller ("my view from this particular bridge," 180); and poet cummings ("Mr. Death," 192). Albee again addresses the difference between the death event and the dying process by having Himself change Hamlet's single act of consummation to "a progression devoutly to be wished" from farm to "first city on the way to others, larger, more distant" (159), a distance that allows one to close down and await literal death. Before the arm, Himself's characterization of the American Dream (perhaps resonant with Albee's Young Man, an angel of death in his first incarnation) is a fantasy of progress unto death: "a lovely wife, some decent kids, a fine home, a rewarding and well-paying career, the respect of my community and a painless, sleeping death" (183).

Albee continues to call attention to theatrical convention. Similar to Annabel in *Lolita*, he has Woman as Himself's mother announce, "We died," to which Himself's father responds, "Well, of course! Why not?"—a bloodless nicety he repeats to distance himself from the stark realities of love and death (157-9). Himself admits, "I have compressed time a little—for the sake of the narrative," (159) and calls attention to the intermission convention. Himself has many long, storytelling speeches in an open lecture hall, and Himself's entrance before his name is announced keeps the convention of abstract character names intact for this play. Note that with Man and Woman Albee has again removed the articles from his abstract character names, and the articles will only return for The Boy in *Three Tall Women* and The Man in *Occupant*.

The Man Who Had Three Arms marks a turning point in Albee's approach to stories or memoirs onstage. *The Ballad of the Sad Café* featured a narrator speaking outside of the episodic scenes to assist in telling Miss Amelia's story. Malcolm's story was told entirely through scenes without narration. The experimental nature of *Mao* gave Long-Winded Lady permission to tell her story without accompanying scenes. In *Lolita*, Humbert participated in the scenes that alternated with his narration. Now, in *The Man Who Had Three Arms*, Man and Woman are subsumed into Himself's memoir, briefly playing all roles required. Himself plays with them but never completely leaves the present moment of his narration, which makes the play more climactic than episodic, especially given the linear progression of Himself's story that occurs without a change of scene and the plot twist that ends the play. From this point forward, Albee is willing to let extended conversation or narration carry the plays in which personal stories dominate the action, rather than presenting those stories in episodic scenes. The three tall women tell their story through conversation in the second act of their play. *Fragments* is primarily the anecdotes of eight characters peppered with interjections. And the entirety of *Occupant* is an interview with Nevelson. In *Listening*, the characters' contests of will are more central to the action than the stories told, but in *The Play About the Baby*, the long narratives sustain the tension of the action that is then released at the end of each act.

FINDING THE SUN

Finding the Sun

In our relationships, the heat of our desires, our hope for help and to be held, is rarely met with a satisfying offer; but the only response to this situation is to go on, enduring life's cycles of heat and cold, finding the sun a temporary respite for our hopelessness.

I. Heat (*3CP 199-211*)

The play opens with four pairs of characters—Abigail and husband Benjamin, Cordelia and husband Daniel, Edmee and son Fergus, Gertrude and husband Henden—entering in turn and finding a spot on the beach in the sun. The opening culminates in a choral "Ahhh-hhhhhh!" from everyone. Throughout the play, relationships across the pairs are revealed or initiated: Benjamin and Daniel were lovers; Gertrude strikes up a conversation with Edmee; Abigail confronts Cordelia; Fergus, the youngest, speaks with Henden, the eldest; Abigail laments her outsider status and the loss of her family to Fergus; Gertrude is Cordelia's mother, and Henden is Daniel's father; Fergus plays catch with Benjamin and Daniel; and Edmee fantasizes about going underwater to Abigail. Edmee praises the "healing heat" of the sun, "the source of all life," but notes the need for "time in the sun *and* time away." "Everything comparative; everything in season" (201-2).

II. Help (*3CP* 211-223)

The frequent use of repeated phrases like "Find the sun" (199) and Cordelia's "The two of you are as close now as you ever were" (213) and Benjamin's "Oh God!" (214-5) give the play a choral quality. Death and dying continue to be thematic motifs in Albee's plays. Edmee's husband drowned (213), and Abigail tells Fergus the strange story of her parents' deaths (222-3). Henden, in a speech to the audience, confides that he is frightened about dying and wonders at what age we become aware of our dying. Henden warily notes that average life spans predict he'll have a few more years to live: "That's a help, though it isn't a guarantee" (215-6). Abigail chides Benjamin with "*You* don't help" (214), and Benjamin chides Daniel and Cordelia with "You guys are no help" (218).

III. Hope (*3CP* 224-237)

The frequent repetition of words and phrases continues with Gertrude's "Mark my words!" and Cordelia's "Oh Mother!" (225-6); "fun!" from Daniel and Benjamin (227), variations on "You guys are *fun!*" from Fergus (227-9), and other repetitions from all three (230); Henden's "What a nice boy" (231-2); and Edmee's "Maybe" (233). Edmee's assertion that "there is no light without dark" (202) plays out here as: there is no hope without loss. Edmee's pride in Fergus is balanced by a fear that he will "turn out...less than he promises" (232). Daniel, lamenting his separation from Benjamin to Henden, cries, "There is no hope! There is…going *on*; there is…getting through it!" (235) To Benjamin's "It's hope-less, then," Daniel says, "It's hope-less, then. What did Beckett say?: I can't go on; I'll go on?" (245-6) Daniel cites the final words of Beckett's novel *The Unnameable*; his father, Henden, speaking of getting older, cites the first words of Beckett's play *Waiting for Godot*: "Nothing to be done" (216). Edmee speaks of categories of sadness, of "tearing loss at Christmas with all my lovelies around me [cf. *All Over*, *2CP* 325-6], implausible sadness on a summer day, but only here, where the earth and water meet, do I feel this…tristesse" (236). Edmee's fantasy of walking into the water is resonant of Charlie in *Seascape*.

IV. Hold (*3CP* 237-248)

Benjamin holds Abigail, but there is no heat: "*You* hold me! But I hardly know it's *you*" (238). After Abigail dares the sun to go out, the "*sun goes behind a cloud*" to initiate the play's final scene, in which Abigail attempts to drown herself, Fergus is missing, and Henden is found to be dead (dimmed light also signals Grandma's departure in both her plays). Albee orchestrates a tone shift as powerful as the one that closes *Virginia Woolf*, rarely permitting the remaining five characters to speak more than eight words at a time, their repetitive lamentations—including Benjamin's "Hold me?" and Edmee's "Fergus?"—countered by Gertrude's "He'll come back my dear; they do. Look! The sun's returning. What glory! What…wonder!"

All the adults at the end of the play are experiencing loss or the pain of unrequited love. Edmee calls fearfully for the absent Fergus; Gertrude and Daniel grieve the death of Henden; Abigail has tried to drown herself; her husband, Benjamin, longs for his former lover,

Daniel. Daniel's wife, Cordelia, is the one who best faces stark reality. Her union with Daniel "isn't *exactly* your usual marriage." She says, "I think I have a friend, and if one day he thinks that our being married is as silly as it *is*…well, then I'll lose the marriage, but I think I'll still have a very good friend" (226). It is Cordelia who comforts Benjamin at the end of the play. Gertrude is in her third marriage, being twice widowed (203); and Henden remarried after the death of his wife of 46 years (207). Daniel is Cordelia's second husband (225). There is parent-child tension between Gertrude and Cordelia (225-6) and between Henden and Daniel (233-5). Daniel's "dearest man, whom I love above all creatures" and his embrace of his father is one of only two tender father-son exchanges in the Albee canon; the other exchange, in *The Goat,* is resonant (from Ross's perspective) with Edmee's characterization of Fergus as having a parental "attachment [that] transcends the usual, the socially *admitted* usual, that is" (214). Cordelia reality-checks Abigail with "What do you *really expect*?" before asserting in reference to Benjamin, "A leopard doesn't change its spots" (205; cf. Gertrude's "skin of a turtle" and Daniel's imagined whale and shark, 243-4). Daniel laments to his father the choice to go against his identity that he has likely made for his father's sake: "There is my *nature* and *Benjamin's* nature, and we are doing what we *can* about it, though I think we're *idiots*" (235). Fergus desires anonymity to explore his identity, a chance to experience "corrupting influences" "without the peril of observation and revelation" (224). Does his disappearance at the end of the play signify that he is taking that chance?

As usual, this play is seasoned with witticisms (often in dark moments) and linguistic quibbles: the "dwell on"/"dwell *in*" joke (202); "she took it into her head to die" of "a brain tumor" (207); "whistling in the…light" (215); "can" corrected to "may" (216); Daniel's "three men and a tub," which Cordelia counters with "Don't be witty" (217); Fergus's emendation of WASP to ASP "to be precise," doubting "there are any black Anglo-Saxons" (224); Edmee's "no, I described it as I intended" (236) and "I wondered if you were *asleep*" not awake (240); and Cordelia's description of Abigail's rescue: "They have her over a barrel—literally; they're pumping the water out of her" (246). Direct address to the audience is limited to three speeches in this play, from Henden (215-6), Fergus (224), and Cordelia (225-6). Albee continues to acknowledge options in his stage directions, as in "*Ignoring? Not having heard?*" (202) and "*Reading? Sunning?*" (211)

In addition to the Beckett references, there is a reference to Wilder ("Grover's Corners," 224), and Gertrude's reference to Shakespeare's "who is *Sylvia*?" (203) is another signpost for *The Goat* up ahead (Gertrude and Cordelia are of course famous Shakespearean names, too). Of young Fergus, Edmee says, "There's danger is consciousness, in too much awareness," to which Henden counters, "[B]etter alert than... numb, or not comprehending" (231). About twenty years after this play was written, David Foster Wallace—whose concerns resonate with those of the Absurdists, e.g.: "How to keep from going through your comfortable, prosperous, respectable, adult life dead, unconscious, a slave to your head and to your natural default setting of being uniquely, completely, imperially alone, day in and day out" (Wallace *TIW* 60)— explores the idea that "consciousness is nature's nightmare" in his book of stories, *Oblivion* (Wallace *OB* 282), in which characters struggle with crippling self-consciousness, the best palliative for which is the alertness required by attempts to reach your fellow man or woman, attempts that are still quite difficult. "[I]nside you is this enormous room full of what seems like everything in the universe at one time or another and yet the only parts that get out have to somehow squeeze out through one of those tiny keyholes you see under the knob in older doors. As if we are all trying to see each other through these tiny keyholes" (Wallace *OB* 178). Henden says that at his age he is frightened and alone, and tapping his head he says, "Nobody gets in there with you" (215).

Finding the Sun has a sense of ritual about it with its repetitive refrains, especially in the sequence of short speeches that serve as the play's climax. Although there are 21 scenes, they *"flow into one another without pause"* (198). It is a lovely, sad, fun, lyrical play whose culminating center is the need to go on finding the sun. It is the third and last of Albee's plays to be set on a beach. Although the character names are not abstracted, they are paired A with B, C with D, E with F, and G with H. The character names in Albee's next play are not abstracted, either, but the names Jack and Gillian resonate with those of the iconic nursery-rhyme couple.

MARRIAGE PLAY

Marriage Play

As in *Finding the Sun*, "going on" in *Marriage Play* is considered hopeless, but it's "what you do" (*3CP* 305). The play is concerned with the effect of routine on identity and with how nothing changes even though everything changes (290) and with how "[a] lot of things are predictable...but very little is certain" (305).

I. Revelation (*3CP* 252-279)

After experiencing a "revelation" (277), Jack comes home and announces, "I'm leaving you," to Gillian, his wife of thirty years (264, 272, 303). In their subsequent banter—which includes quibbles over definitions and usage—the frequently asked question "What do you mean?" also has a hint of philosophical resonance given Jack's crisis of identity born of monotony at work: "You look up one day from your desk; you are sitting there in your usual manner, doing your usual things—and they are neither boring nor exciting: whatever they may have been they no longer are; they are merely my usual things" (254). "You realize your life is about to change…profoundly" (255). Gillian mocks Jack's narrative and then says, "[Y]ou have the most predictable crises; you should read more" (258). Jack's tactic for getting Gillian to "pay proper attention" to his revelation of an impending change of routine is to initiate a routine of going out and coming back in again. Gillian avoids the generalization and abstraction of routine by recording specific details in what she calls *The Book of Days*: "Every time we have made love I have notated it here; I have commented on it—duration, positions, time of day, necessity, degrees of enjoyability, snatches of conversation, the weather" (264). When Jack asks her to read from the book, she asks him to "choose a number" and then says of his choice of eight hundred "so…rounded, so…predictable" before reading the entry: "Will he never learn?!" (265) He uses less rounded numbers in his subsequent requests for readings.

When Jack maligns Gillian's book, she defends it as "a record of our touching" (267). Man 4 in *Fragments* laments lives lived "without touching" (455), although he is referring to general human contact rather than to contact between spouses. The tone of Gillian's rhyme— "Sad husband, sad wife; Sad day; sad life" (258)—recalls "George and Martha: sad, sad, sad" (*1CP* 277). Gillian uses baby talk like Martha, and Jack deflects Gillian with "Quite a performance," as George does Martha (*3CP* 279, cf. *1CP* 289). Jack's reference to a grandmother with a Pekingese (*3CP* 274) recalls Grandma in *The American Dream*. Gillian's reference to "the boy you were in love with when you were thirteen" (290) recalls Jerry's "jazz of a very special hotel" (*1CP* 24). Unlike Peter, whose misunderstanding of Jerry is honest, Gillian uses "I understand" (*3CP* 278) to mock and reject Jack's story of his revelation (276-7).

II. This Is What You Do (*3CP 279-306*)

Gillian says, "[Y]ou didn't come here this afternoon to share anything; you didn't come home here this afternoon to be understood; you came home here this afternoon to make an announcement and then get out as fast as you could!" (280) Jack and Gillian engage in an epic physical fight (282-3), resonant in intensity with the battle that closes *The Ballad of the Sad Café*, although here Jack and Gillian fight in private and afterwards compliment one another and resume their verbal fight over topics relevant to their marriage: lost potential, memory, betrayal, inevitable failure, routine. Of Jack's putative departure, Gillian says, "I've missed you for years, and so why not now" (285). This recalls Gillian's speech about how it does no good to be herself, after which she calls Jack a "[nine negative adjectives] memory of the man I prayed would want me" (272-3). Now, daring Jack to leave, she says, "You're not big enough for the gesture. You're...*nothing*" (286). Jack laments the loss of his youthful "glow." Their exchange—

> GILLIAN: Nothing changes.
>
> JACK: *Everything* changes.
>
> GILLIAN: Which is therefore the same thing, blah blah blah. (290)

—resonates with the statements about truth that close *The Lady from Dubuque* (*2CP* 667-8). Gillian challenges Jack's memory, and then at his request to "Think about the good times" she recounts a liaison in Venice that she realizes during the telling is not a memory of Jack. Jack laments that his frequent infidelities cause Gillian to experience pain and mistrust, to which she says "Once is all it takes" (*3CP* 294-8). To Jack's claim "it means nothing," she counters "To whom?" (300) Jack and Gillian each accuse the other of not listening. Gillian says, "Your mind is always cocked for something else... I see it in your eyes; I see you not listen" (301), which recalls both *Listening* and the idea of the eyes as a measure of connection in *All Over* and *The Man Who Had Three Arms*.

Countering Jack, Gillian says, "Passion in a marriage never dies; it changes. When the passion of passion wanes there are all the others waiting to rush in—the passion of loss, of hatred, the passion of indifference; the ultimate, the finally satisfying passion of nothing" (302). Jack says, "We stare into the dark and know that nothing is enough,...that the failure is built into us, that the greatest awareness gives to the greatest dark. That I'm going to lose you, for example—*have* lost you—no more, no less than fingers slipping from each other, that I'm going to lose *me*, *have* lost me—the light...losing the light." This equates despair with a loss of light as in *Finding the Sun*, and Gillian echoes *Seascape* when she says "we've got some life left in us" (303). Jack uses the phrase "Irrevocably intertwined" to mock the dependency of marriage, but Gillian counters that marriage should not put identity in crisis, "that marriage does *not* make two people one, it makes two people two—a good marriage, a useful marriage—makes individuals! That when two people choose to be together though they're strong enough to be alone, *then* you have a good marriage....With any luck we've not compensated, we've complimented. Well, at least that's how it's supposed to go" (304). Of routine she says, "A lot of things are predictable—you, for example, and everything about you—but very little is certain" (305).

While there are no overt references to theatrical conventions or playwrights here, nods to both Miller's *Death of a Salesman* and Beckett's *Waiting for Godot* close the play (cf. Zinman, 114-7). Jack has exhorted Gillian to "pay proper attention" throughout the play, which echoes Albee's *Listening* and Miller's "attention must be paid" (Miller 188). The futility of Jack's annual planting of a garden echoes Willy's actions near the end of

Miller's play. But as Gillian says, "This is what you do." There is a hint of hopefulness in Gillian's "scatter some seeds.....*Something* will come up." But then Jack says again, "I'm leaving you," and as at the end of Beckett's play, there is *"no movement"* (305-6).

Gillian suggests that a good marriage promotes individual identity (304). When Jack suggests, in reference to Gillian's writing style, "[T]ry being you," she counters by defending the consistency of her identity against Jack's inattention: "I've tried that, sweetie; it doesn't work. I've tried it for thirty years. Give me another suggestion" (272-3). Of Jack's threat to leave her, she says, "Have you forgotten who you are? Who I am?" (279) While animal instinct generally refers to a sexual impulse here (270, 272, 298), Jack speaks of instinct below the veneer of civilization, too (301). There is also the impulse to deny reality: Gillian says, to counter Jack's assertion of leaving, "I shall pretend otherwise" (285); they speak of "the people we pretended to be" on their first date (294); Jack, to counter Gillian's "you'll believe anything," says, "Sometimes we *want* to" (300); Gillian says of infidelity that Jack can "pretend it's love when it's really desperate" (303). But Gillian acknowledges Jack's realistic assertion "that nothing is enough," "that the failure is built into us, that the greatest awareness gives to the greatest dark" (303).

Jack says of his revelation at the office, "I become aware of awareness I have never known," and speaks of levitating to observe himself (276-7). In David Foster Wallace's *The Pale King*, a 2011 novel also concerned with staying present amid routine, Shane Drinion levitates "when his attention is completely on something else," when he listens intently to his colleague Meredith Rand (Wallace, *TPK* 485). Here, Gillian's self-awareness is also enhanced by another, by Jack's touch as described in event twenty-six in Gillian's *The Book of Days* (271).

Albee's characters continue to be aware of linguistic choices, meanings, and distortions. Conversation turns on the definition of "dalliance" and the applicability of that word to Jack's infidelity (253-4). Jack chooses to end a sentence with an adverb rather than a preposition (254). Because thoughts are silent, Jack qualifies "you say to yourself" with "so to speak," an accurate idiom even though used to indicate not actually speaking (255, 277). Gillian ambiguously answers "Yes" when Jack asks two questions in rapid sequence (255). Jack counters Gillian's "May I help you?"—an attempt to play a character in the narrative of his revelation—with "Don't help" (255). There's a quibble over "profoundest" versus "most profound" (255-6). Gillian exhorts Jack to "[b]e *precise*" and then upon his exit quips, "You have done everything at least once too often" (260). She uses "nearly" to keep Jack accurate (264) and amends "who" to "whom" (273). In the aftermath of their fight, they wonder whether hydrophobia is the same as rabies (284-5). Gillian distorts "tangled web" to "wangled teb" (293). For the first time since *Listening*, no characters address the audience. Albee still addresses the production team in his stage directions, saying of a magazine Gillian throws at Jack, "*It hits him, or it does not, preferable does*" (257). Several authors are referenced here: Hemingway, James, Lawrence, Melville, Pope (266, 271, 272, 281, 291).

The play, featuring a pair of characters whose names recall the iconic nursery-rhyme pair, is concerned with a sense of hopelessness or loss of identity in the face of routine, centering around and culminating in Jack's recurring "I'm leaving you." (There are three Jacks in the Albee canon; no other specific name is used as often for characters that appear in the plays.) The fight in the center of the play is less of a climax than a turning point that starts us on a path back to where we started: "I'm leaving you." Most of Jack's monologue of his revelation at work is a repetition of what he's previously told Gillian. Gillian's speech about changing passions and the "passion of nothing" (302) is countered by Jack's speech about loss and how "nothing is enough"

(303). Gillian asserts that the routine of marriage does not compromise identity: "[W]e've not become each other; we've become ourselves" (304). While the play is set in a "*suburban home*" (251), the sense of confinement springs more from routine and feelings of loss than from environment.

THREE TALL WOMEN

Three Tall Women

Albee continues to concern himself with the idea of going on through life's obstacles. In *Three Tall Women*, he gives us an extended example of how one goes on living and how perspective and identity can change throughout the span of one's life, examining points A, B, and C of a particular life that draws inspiration from Albee's adoptive mother.

I. How She Goes On (*3CP* 310-351)

In the first act, B is A's caretaker, and C is from A's lawyer's office. C characterizes A's assertion that A is one year younger than C's papers indicate as vanity; B characterizes it as forgetting (310; Albee specifies ages for B and C—52 and 26—but not for the elder A, 309). C's "Why would you lie about one *year*?" prompts clucks from B and A: "How you go *on*" (314). Though "go on" here means "extend speech unnecessarily," the play provides an example of how one goes on through the hopelessness of life, one of Albee's signature concerns, as is his interest in linguistic games. To A's "I want to go," C quips, "On?" to play on the immediate conversation, but the exchange could also articulate the question of whether the aging A wants to die or go on living; actually she just wants to go to the bathroom. C sarcastically calls attention to the importance of numerical specificity with her "or five, or seven" game (314, 319, 337), but when B amends C's "him" to "he" (cf. "shook" to "shaken," 338), C retorts "Yes; I know" (312), which implies that she does not consider grammatical accuracy as "important" (311) as numerical accuracy.

Albee's interest in awareness of the dying process is especially apt in this play, the second act of which looks at stages of an entire life all at once. B says, "You start...and then you stop....I'd like to see children learn it.... Make 'em aware they're dying from the minute they're alive" (318). Albee frequently associates decline with an image of going downhill: here (317, 380), in *The Man Who Had Three Arms* (148), and in *The Goat* (555). Three times Albee's husbands—George in *Virginia Woolf*, Richard in *Everything in the Garden*, and Jack in *Marriage Play*—have characterized their wives' passionate, heartfelt expressions as performance. Here, C characterizes A's petulant vulnerability as "a production" (320). As usual, Albee doesn't soften the ugliness of prejudice. Across the generations here, C is offended by and B apologizes for A's blatant insensitivity (331, 334-5, 340, 343). B says that "it doesn't *mean* anything. It's the way she learned things." If B had stopped a sentence earlier, C could have countered with "To whom?" as Gillian did to Jack's justification of infidelity (300). Albee does have B use that tactic here when B moves C's attention from A to B with "For whom?" (317). A refers to show boys as "fairies" (342), and in a chilling slip that reveals the inheritance of self-detrimental ideas, C (in the second act) asserts that diamonds are "tangible proof…that we're valuable…(*Embarrassed*) that we're valued" (379).

A's stories of her life experience begin to dominate the narrative. Her relation of these is nonlinear, moving from her mother's advice to her upon leaving home, to her quick courtship, to riding horses and accruing money after marriage, forward to recent doctor visits and memory problems and suspicions, back to riding and her husband's injury, back to childhood, and then to life in the city with Sis. A chides, "[Sis] always thought everything would fall right into her lap. And it *did*; a *lot*…I had to work for everything nothing came my way" (341), before telling an uncomfortable story, the memory of which brings her to tears, of a necklace offered by her husband to entice oral sex. When she declined—"You *know* I can't *do* that!"—her husband went from erect to flaccid, causing the necklace to fall "deep into my lap. Keep it, he said" (347). Upon being helped to her bed, A speaks of struggling with her memory. She remembers being tall and the gifts she's received from her son. She hints at the later pieces of her story that will be told in the second act before going silent and still. Fearing A has had a stroke, C exits to call A's son, and B exits to call A's doctor.

II. And So It Goes (*3CP* 352-384)

Albee makes one of his boldest, most original dramatic choices for the second act of this play: B and C become 52-year-old A and 26-year-old A; and A—"*sling gone*" (354, cf. 315) and "*thoroughly rational during this Act*" (354)—soon joins B and C to reflect on her life from different vantage points, while "A," a dummy with a breathing mask dressed as A was in the first act, remains propped up in the bed (352). Roudané notes that this second act "presents a death watch scenario, reminiscent of *All Over*" (Roudané 139). Albee signals the change to the shared character in the dialogue. B resumes the topic of dying and ways to die, suggesting that intruders might "slit your throat, my throat.... All that blood on the Chinese rug....We get it at auction." To C's "I wouldn't know," A counters, "You will, though—the rug, I mean. Clearly nobody slits your throat, or mine, for that matter" (*3CP* 353). The shared characterization was foreshadowed in the first act. To C's "There's *nothing* the matter with me," A retorts, "[Y]ou just *wait*" (321). A also says of C, "[S]he'll learn" (323, 325), and B says of C, "[Y]ou'll get there" (349). Albee's playful stage directions also signal the merger:

> A ("*Come off it*"): Oh, *really.*
> B ("*Oh, really*"): Come *off* it. (355)

C speaks to the audience (355), signaling her takeover of A's narrative from the first act (in which no one spoke to the audience). B signals her takeover of the narrative by speaking to the audience, too (372). A eventually resumes the narrative (375) and speaks to the audience to close the play (384).

A and B bring a different perspective to C's innocent flirtation narrative, recalling "a little calculation; a little design" (357). Also, A can now look at her relationship with her son dispassionately, whereas B, who shouts "Get out of my house!" when he enters (369), cannot. This is a reversal of the situation at the end of the first act, when B counters A's lament "He never comes to see me" with "he's a good son" (350). Mocking C's rejection of the news that her father will die, B says, "[S]he loves me; how can I go and die on her?" (366) It was C who was incredulous in the first act, countering A's complaint about the contract of friendship with "What right do they have to die?" (337) There is one potential discrepancy between the acts. Informing C about her future husband, B says, "[H]e's divorcing his second wife; she's just plain bad;

the first one drank; still does" (365). But A says this in the first act: "[T]he first one was a whore, the second one was a drunk" (323).

Several of Albee's recurring images and concerns crop up as the women tell their story. C relates a brief, early romantic encounter (358), a motif that began with Jerry (C's story includes a revelation—an attempt at oral sex which leads to throwing up (360)—that helps us see the necklace story in a new light). Infidelity, a major concern of *Marriage Play*, is succinctly examined here (364). A's mother lived with her and kept Pekingese dogs (367) like Grandma. The son becomes an absent child for twenty years (371). A's fall from her horse is seen as lost potential in the eyes of others: "[O]nce you fall…they won't hate you quite so much…because you're not perfect" (377). Of the effects of her husband's cancer, A says, "[I]t's all downhill from there" (380). B says of aging, "[T]hat doesn't mean closing down" (383).

C triggers a summation of each of the three perspectives to close the play when she asks "What about the happy times…the *happiest* moments?" (382) The play comes full circle when C amends B's statement of her age (as C amended A to begin the play) and B responds (as C did to B's grammar amendment in the first act) "Yes, I know" (383). A's discussion of being beside herself and thinking of herself "in the third person" is underscored by "A" being in bed onstage and by the three perspectives being explored in the second act. A says that the happiest moment is "When we stop. When we can stop" (384). This recalls B's summation of life and dying in the first act: "You start…and then you stop" (318).

Lament for compromised desire is a recurring motif in *Three Tall Women*. B says, "It's downhill from sixteen on!" and "You can't get your way in the world," and A says of her husband, "[H]e was wonderful, but then there's life" (317, 353, 361). A, B, and C discuss their family bonds and conflicts, especially between mother and 20-years-absent son. The play explores how time as well as relationships can shape identity. A informs B that in reality B will change her mind regarding her son, that even a strained relationship is better than isolation: "Be alone except for her upstairs passed out on the floor, and the piano top with the photos in the silver frames, and the butler, and…be all alone; you *do* want to see him again, but the terms are too hard. We never forgive him. We let him come, but we never forgive him" (371). B feels betrayed not just by the boy's departure but by his crass evocation of her infidelity as a parting shot (374). The eroticism of the horse-and-groom story (373) recalls *Tiny Alice* (*1CP* 497-500), and C makes an "*Animal growl of protest*" (*3CP* 353). Roudané notes that "Albee mentions Dalmations, Pekingese, cats, ponies, horses, jaybirds, buzzards, and penguins" (Roudané 138). Of the avoidance of reality, B says that she'll watch A "*pretend* to handle" her own affairs (*3CP* 332). In the second act, C avoids the reality of who she will become: B and A. B is angered over being sheltered by adults from stark reality: "You're growing up and they go out of their way to hedge, to qualify, to…to evade; to avoid, to *lie*. Never tell how it is—how it's *going* to be—when a half-truth can be got in there" (372). A embraces the reality of "Coming to the end of it": "There's a difference between knowing you're going to *die* and *knowing* you're going to die. The second is better; it moves away from the theoretical" (384).

In addition to B's grammatical emendations, B cites A's use of a "figure of speech" (318), and A interrogates B's use of a cliché (360-1). The characters' awareness of the audience is delayed until the second act to underline the expansion of consciousness in that act. Albee continues to tie the present realities of the audience and characters together with stage directions: "It's [*whatever day it is in reality*]" (311, 322; cf. "[*Ibid.*]," 312). There are no direct theatrical references here, but Zinman suggests a kinship between this play and Beckett's *Rockaby* (Zinman 122-4). A's brief ritual of denials prompts the summation of perspectives that close the play, speeches matched only by B's recounting of her son's departure (373-4). A, B, and C are the most abstracted names in the Albee canon, and these names allow for the characters to be different people in the first act and the same person in the second act. Albee hasn't used "very much like" in a while, but he does say that B "*Looks rather as A would have at 52*" and that C "*Looks rather as B would have at 26*" (309). The environment of this play is confined to a bedroom, but simultaneous perspectives on an entire life are able to be considered, the living and dying of A, B, and C being the culminating center of the play.

FRAGMENTS

Fragments

In 1961, Esslin says that "the masses who live from day to day...have lost all contact with the basic facts—and mysteries—of the human condition with which, in former times, they were kept in touch through the living ritual of their religion, which made them parts of a real community and not just atoms in an atomized society" (Esslin 400). In 1993, Albee's octet of atoms becomes a molecular community simply by sitting around (Albee subtitled the play *A Sit-Around* in response to critics declaring that it was not a play, *3CP* 386) and speaking aloud fragments of individual thoughts and experiences, often expressing a desire to help by doing so, a community that, although not tension-free, is willing to reach their fellow man—to literally engage in a ritual of touching someone who wants to be touched (*3CP* 455). The play concludes with a call to consciousness of both the futility and wonder of life via participation in that life (*3CP* 456), which recalls the Absurdist credo that "life must be faced in its ultimate, stark reality" (Esslin 401).

I. Everything Helps (*3CP* 389-430)

Esslin says that "communication between human beings is… often shown in a state of breakdown in the Theatre of the Absurd," because the language that we use conceals authentic content. The "ossified clichés that dominate thought" must be "replaced by a living language" and "the uses of poetic language acknowledged" (Esslin 409-10). *Fragments* begins and ends with eight characters (four men and four women aged 20s-60s) sharing proverbs (clichés' cousins). The last proverb spoken before Man 4 gathers the books from which they are read, and which Woman 4 calls "the best one," is "Dunder do gally the beans" (*3CP* 392). This proverb inspires acknowledgement of uncertainty and creativity. Man 4 then invites the others to make up a proverb, and Man 2 volunteers an original poem that seems to be about the thrill of challenging imagination and perspective. The proverbs attempt to convey essential, objective wisdom about common human experience. They also serve as points of connection and conversation starters (more inviting than, say, "I've been to the zoo") and as a gateway to exchanges of more subjectivity that challenge imagination and perspective. Each of the eight characters will share fragments of their individual thoughts and experiences that, like the proverbs, are intended to help but that, given their uniqueness, are hard to codify into essential, objective phrases.

Man 4 begins with a fragment that is not his own. He announces to the others: "Edward Albee, who wrote this play, wanted you to know about this charity auction—a sort of celebrity auction he was asked to participate in" (396). In a play that features characters building community through personal revelation, this might be Albee sharing something personal, or he might have made it up. Albee's biographer relates that at least two of the other fragments are derived from Albee's personal experience (Gussow 348-50) but doesn't mention a celebrity auction. Regardless, the anecdote is about gaining perspective on others' perceptions of one's worth, although the perspective in this case is derived from bids on celebrity-decorated eggs.

Man 3 then describes his dream of an *avant-garde*, ritualistic theatre piece. Albee indirectly puts himself in this fragment by having Woman 1, a great fan of musical theatre, express in a cheerful way Albee's less favorable opinion of musicals, referenced here not as the *apres-garde* but the *derriere-guard*. Man 3's dream prompts Woman 4, the eldest woman, to lament, "Things vanish sometimes like in dreams and we're not even aware they're gone, or that they ever were—that we used to be around them and take them for granted" (406). She gives knife grinders as an example of "all the little things people set themselves out to do then. How much more...community there was" (409). Continuing the idea of challenging awareness, Woman 3 describes her recent annual checkup in which her doctor suggests that parts of her body—fallopian tubes, kidneys, breasts—have been reversed. Albee's motif of challenging the veneer of civilization returns when Man 1 wonders why "we do some things together and some things we don't," using the equally important "eating and shitting" as an example (412). Of the social aspects of eating, Woman 3 says, "They call it civilization" (413). Man 3 upholds the veneer with "there's a reason for everything; don't...trouble yourself" (415).

In the introduction to Woman 2's story of the burial of her dog (one of the anecdotes from Albee's life that Gussow relates), there is reference to Bush Junior being worse than Bush Senior (417), which indicates that Albee updated his original 1993 text before publication of the play in the collected edition of 2005. The fact that Donald Trump is just a celebrity here (399) and not more lamented than Bush Junior locks the play into a time before the Trump presidency, so for a contemporary production I would suggest cutting the original Trump reference and replacing Bush Senior with Bush Junior and Bush Junior with Trump. Woman 2 has to tell Man 2 that she's not done with her story; this recalls Man 2 having to announce there was a second stanza to his poem (394). Man 3's revelation of another person in his mirror "seeing through me to himself" (425) is an idea Albee develops into his last published play, for which Man 3 also provides the title: "me, myself and I" (424). The burial of Woman 2's dog prompts a memory of Woman 1's cremated cat that she is conflicted about telling. Woman 3 suggests, "It might help" to tell it. Pausing mid-story, Woman 1 asks, "Do I have to?" when prompted to continue and then immediately says, "I have to!!" when given the chance to stop. It turns out she may have confused which ashes were her cat's and which were her friend's, perhaps sprinkling the ashes in the wrong places. Man 4 asks, "What can it possibly matter?" before calling for an intermission.

II. Participate (*3CP* 431-457)

The actors return; Man 4 announces "Act Two" and asks if Woman 1 is feeling better; and Man 1 launches into the longest speech of the play. In the prelude to his tale, he asserts, "People want me," which resonates with what Young Man says to Grandma: "I let people touch me" (*1CP* 139). The tale proper recalls *Lolita* in that Man 1's neighbor is consumed with lust for his 13-year-old daughter, but "since she is filled with an innocence, a purity commensurate with my lust, transcending it," he, unlike Humbert, asks the 15-year-old Man 1— himself kept by a man who "didn't want anything I couldn't give him with my eyes closed"—to defile the daughter and report the sordid details back to the father, who craves loss and despair. The child is moved into her alcoholic aunt's house, where it is anticipated that she easily can be degraded. Man 1, who had no illicit intentions with respect to the daughter—"we were little kids"—lies to the father, consulting the "porno library" of his "protector" for source material. About a month later, Man 1 decides to tell the father the true story of an innocent exchange the previous night, ending with the daughter touching his cheek, which sends the father into a murderous rage. Man 1 leaves town and never sees any of them again: "My cheek still has a warmth to it, though, a glow. I still feel her fingers brushing me. Perhaps it's a wound; perhaps there's a wound there" (*3CP* 432-4).

Man 2 and Woman 1 repeat portions of Man 1's speech in parody, beginning with "People want me," and are gently admonished by Man 4 and Man 3. To Man 1's "You can't say *anything* around here" Woman 3 reassures, "Yes, you *can*; you *can*" (436). Man 2 apologizes and explains what inspired his parody: "If you're black most people don't *want* to see you." Recalling Oscar in *The Lady from Dubuque*, he says, "I'm black? You noticed?" He then shares a brief anecdote of his friend being arrested "for being black, for being in the park" (437). Albee had Oscar, though a powerful entity, sarcastically play on racial stereotypes to mock the other characters. Man 2 calls out Man 4's unnecessary characterization of a couple as black with more grace and less self-deprecation than Oscar: "Black, were they?" (452, 453). Man 4 doesn't realize what Man 2 is doing, which is an example of the generational differences Albee is highlighting in the play (confer Woman 4's knife-grinder fragment in the first act and the sequence about "the way we call things" in this act, 446). Albee's characters are finding common ground across the variables of age, race, and gender, with each character getting equal representation with one anecdote per act. Note two exceptions to this pattern, though. Man 2, the only character out of eight required to be African-American, offers his poem in the first act—which is more the culmination of the proverbs section than a fragment in its own right—and provides only the speech described above as a coda to Man 1's fragment in the second act. Woman 4, the eldest woman, contributes to the conversation in the second act, but has no fragment of her own. Although women are equally represented as characters, the inherent sexism of societal assumptions is represented here, too. Consider "A woman's advice is nothing much, but he who doesn't take it is a fool" (one of Man 2's proverbs, 391) and the "Most shoplifters *are* women" sequence (441).

Whatever tensions may exist between these eight characters fall away though when Man 4 concludes the final fragment before the return to proverbs with "Sometimes I wonder why we all go through our lives without touching one another very much," prompting all of the others to participate in a powerful ritual: "*The others move to touch him; some embrace, some stroke, others just…touch. After they do so they move back to where they were. Take your time with this*" (455). Albee uses the imagery of hands and touching in all the other fragments of the second act, too. Man 1 begins with "people couldn't keep their hands off me" (431); Woman 2 offers information from an article she "thought might be some help" (437), which suggests that the names we "call our mates" are "shorthand signals; they signal our special bond" (438); Man 3's father's justification of his obsessive shoplifting is that he thought the items "might come in handy" (444); Woman 1's justification for talking to her plants is that "it tickles me—doing it" (447); and Woman 3 says of the set piece delivered by a famous old movie star at a party, it was "as if a button had been pushed," "as if someone wound her up" (451).

Albee's motif of the eyes going out, initiated in *All Over*, is evoked in reference to Man 3's mother after the arrest of his father for shoplifting:

"It was as if she'd closed a venetian blind behind her eyes; you couldn't see into her head anymore" (443). Albee's signature concerns with the lifelong process of dying and an insistence that we not close down highlight the end of the play. Consider this exchange between the eldest and youngest men:

> MAN 4: I have gotten to that age when my contemporaries—
> my friends, my loved ones, my acquaintances—are dying
> around me.
> MAN 1: Hanh! Me, too!
> MAN 4: No, I mean what they refer to as a normal death.
> MAN 1: There's no such thing!
> MAN 4 (*Placating*): I know; I know. I mean people my age.
> MAN 1: So do I! (453-4)

Man 4 makes a concluding statement in which he asserts that the way to get through life is to be aware of our limited time—"so long as you know there's doom right from the beginning"—and our agency: "while we may not be responsible for everything that *does* happen to us, we certainly are for everything that *doesn't*," and "since we're conscious, we have to be aware of both the awful futility of [life] and the amazing wonder. Participate, I suppose" (456). Himself, the man who had three arms, conveys similar but darker sentiments: "There is...not a life hasn't seen futility at the end.... No matter how rich the life,...the sense comes that there is nothing except the doing of it" (151; see also Himself's characterization of the man destroyed by and worshipping futility, 152). Man 4 initiates the return to proverbs, and reiterating the necessity of participation, says to the others, "Now you do one." All the other characters repeat an earlier proverb, ending again with the imaginative "Dunder do gally the beans." Man 4 then simply announces the end of play, but I hear this final sequence as an invitation to use the play as a model, if it helps, for reaching other people.

There aren't direct references to our animal natures in this play, but in two of the fragments animals are provided the same burial considerations as people, and when Woman 1 has potentially confused the locations for the spreading of human and animal ashes, Man 4 says, "What can it possibly matter?" The need to gather as a group, true of most animals, is represented, but because this group is not a family, their impulses to bond with and to challenge one another are not influenced by shared pasts. The characters do not question their identities or existence, with the exception of Man 3, who fears that he will vanish when he looks in the mirror (425). The childhood experiences Man 1 describes qualify as damaging, but he, like Lolita, doesn't seem to be traumatized by those experiences. The play concludes with a call to face the reality that we are doomed to die by participating in both the wonder and futility of life.

The audience is only directly addressed in the announcements of the beginning of each act and of the end of the play. These announcements, recalling those of Jerry and of *Ballad*'s Narrator for their stories, signal the audience to look for unity in a play composed of fragments. The play has a self-conscious quality. The first fragment after proverbs begins, "Edward Albee, who wrote this play . . ." (396), and Woman 1 refers to herself asking a question as she asks it: "What do you mean, she said?" (412) Norma Jenckes characterizes this self-consciousness as postmodernist tension. After Man 4's call for participation, Man 3 says with some sarcasm, "Let me write this down" (456). Jenckes notes that Albee has earnest, existential truths that he still wants to enunciate, but he has learned that they will not wash in the late 1990s environment of relativism and disdain. So he places the modernist speech in one character's mouth, but then instantly undercuts it with the postmodernist denigration of another character. This is one way of demonstrating continuing modernist and postmodernist tensions. (Jenckes 113)

This undercutting occurs throughout the play. In his opening stage directions, Albee, with his characteristic awareness of the varied nature of performance, invites both undercutting and support in the opening sequence: "*Between the reading of each proverb, each of the others is requested to make some comment about that proverb if anything comes to mind—ironic, flippant, supportive, whatever. These may vary from performance to performance, but I imagine some of them will become set. Be free with it*" (389). Other examples of undercutting include Woman 4's "Can't you be sensible about anything?" (438), in response to Woman 2's initiation of the fragment about the names we call our mates, and the parody of Man 1's fragment. This fragment highlights an analogous tension between innocence and base cynicism when Man 1 relates an experience of purity in response to his neighbor's craving for pornography.

Albee's interest in linguistic precision and choice is evident here, too. Woman 4 changes "information" to "education" "to be more precise" (408); Woman 2 clarifies "which paw, not which husband" (419); and Man 4 corrects "us men, we men" (451). Woman 4 characterizes "Poor thing!" as "an all-purpose phrase" (426) and is nostalgic for the phrases "Knew it in my bones" and "Out of the blue" (442); perambulator is a "good word" (431); and kleptomaniac is a "Funny word" (440). Albee again uses baby talk (438) and can't resist using "No shit!" in reference to shit (415). Albee embeds a Shakespeare reference in his commentary on musicals—"*full* of sound—not much fury, of course" (403)—and references Lear (455). Albee calls for a "*projected title*" (431) to accompany the announcement of Act Two, but does not ask for a projection in the first act (confer similar meta-theatrical inconsistencies in *Counting the Ways*).

There is a hint of ritual in that the "*Actors return in the reverse order in which they left*" (431), and the play closes with everyone participating in the ritual of touching Man 4. Man 1 delivers another tour-de-force monologue (431-4) in a play rife with interesting stories. Albee again uses abstracted names for all characters, and in terms of environment, *Fragments* is the least-specified play in the canon: "Do *not* be specific about 'where we are' or who the characters 'are'" (387). The play is divided only by the act break and occurs in real time, but its varied content is not linked by cause-and-effect logic, making it, like the previous two plays, difficult to characterize as either climactic or episodic. Potentially helpful proverbs and stories are shared throughout the play, culminating in a call for awareness and participation. Also of interest structurally, Zinman notes:

> Before changing *Fragments'* subtitle to *A Sit-Around*, Albee subtitled it "A Concerto Grosso," a Renaissance musical style in which each instrument takes a solo. This is one of several of Albee's attempts to make drama approach the condition of music, suggesting the vital importance of timing in the performance of an Albee play and the interplay of voices as if they were instruments. (Zinman 128)

THE PLAY ABOUT THE BABY

The Play About the Baby

In *The Play About the Baby*, "Good things to good people and happy endings" are feared to be "a single instant of glory, desperately cruel." "We can't take glory because it shows us the abyss," the pain and loss, the wounds which are inevitable, a prerequisite for adult identity, for "getting through it all" (*3CP* 498). Also, our needs determine our reality, which makes reality a function of the present moment: "[F]irst we *invent*, and then we *reinvent*. As with the past so the future." "What's real and what isn't? Tricky" (468).

I. What's Real and What Isn't? (*3CP* 461-496)

The play begins with Girl announcing, calmly, that she's "going to have the baby now" and then exiting with Boy. There is an extended sequence of labor and birth sounds that take the focus offstage, which hasn't happened since *Bessie* and *Fam and Yam*. Girl and Boy return speaking in tones more flat than celebratory, Girl stating her experience of pain as simply a fact she remembers. The topic of pain prompts Boy's narrative of the time his arm was broken, which is interspersed with sexual banter between Boy and Girl as Girl breastfeeds the baby. Albee instructs, "*We do not see the baby, merely its blanket*" (462). Boy and Girl behave and think more like children or adolescents than adults, Girl even suckling Boy to comfort him over the memory of the pain he felt when his arm was broken. Boy says, as his mouth is on Girl's breast, that one of his attackers "undid his fly, and I don't know what he was going to do" (465). Boy has an idea, but Girl leads him offstage before he can develop and articulate it.

Man enters and speaks at length to the audience. He first takes pleasure in the "youngsmell" that lingers on the chairs, noting later that scent, like all things (like youth) fades. He provides two examples drawn from experiences of time and memory that suggest reality is a function of the present moment: the sense—the reality—that the trip back from a place we've never been before is shorter than the trip to it and the night that he didn't remember that the woman standing in front of him was his mother. Further articulating the dependence of reality on the present moment, he says, "I wonder how I'll remember (*Gestures about him*) all of *this*? But, since I'm not *there* yet—so to speak—have not, haven't remembered it…(*Brisk*) well, first we invent, and then we *re*invent. As with the past so the future." He summarizes by asserting that our reality is determined by our need and that "what's true and what isn't is a tricky business, no? What's real and what isn't? Tricky" (468), introducing Woman as he exits.

Before Woman can introduce herself, Boy enters. Although Boy doesn't recognize Woman, he speaks—in "Hyperbole"—about Girl's body and his exploration of it. Girl calls him back, echoing Man's temporal awareness and adding spatial and sexual resonances: "you're not there yet" (471). Woman explains that she is here to assist Man. She shares that she used to be married to a man who wouldn't eat dinner with her, even when she became a good cook in an attempt to change that situation. She relates an attempt to interview a writer "to try to comprehend the 'creative mind' as they call it" and is interrupted by Boy chasing Girl across stage, contrasting what will be a successful physical chase with Woman's unsuccessful intellectual chase of an understanding of another's subjective creativity. Man returns, noting "How innocent they are" before leaving again with Woman. Boy and Girl return, alternating confusion about who Woman is with sexual banter, at first innocent but then turning darker as Boy urges Girl offstage to do something new, using "*mock eloquence*" (quickly and obviously dropped) as a manipulative tactic.

Man enters and speaks of the time he pretended to be blind at "a sculpture exhibit set up especially for the blind," noting how the blind experience reality through touch and how "very different" it felt to touch with his eyes closed the penis of the copy of the "famous bronze sculpture of the wild boar in Florence" than it did to touch the original with his eyes open. Man asks the audience, "Have you seen the baby? Cute, no?" But of course we haven't seen (or touched) the baby; we do hear the baby crying offstage after being born (461), and we hear its offstage cries of hunger (462, 487). Man, recalling his earlier assertion that reality is based on need, continues, "I wonder how much they love it? How much they need it?" (479) Reality is also determined by per-suasion. Boy, responding to Girl's displeasure with what Boy wanted to try, says, "Sorry. (*Not really*)," but then after Girl's "Mean it!" Boy says, "(*Genuine*) Sorry" (480). This recalls Jerry asking Peter "Do you mind if we talk?" and then twice responding to Peter's "No" with "Yes you do," before Peter decides, "I don't mind at all, really" (*1CP* 17). It also foreshadows Man and Woman's extended persuasion of Girl and Boy about a real child at the end of the play, which in turn recalls George's extended persuasion of Martha about an imaginary child at the end of their play (cf. *SMM* 289).

Boy tells the story of seeing Girl on a stretcher and following her to the hospital, thinking that upon waking "she'll love me," a situation foretold to Girl by a Gypsy who spoke of "the boy you would marry." Boy corrects himself with respect to time when he says "I assumed you weren't—wouldn't be" dead and then says "It's easy to foretell the future: you just have to know what's going to happen." But when Girl asked the Gypsy if she and Boy would have a baby, the Gypsy said, "I can't see that...besides: your time is up." Boy asserts, "Gypsies steal babies!" and provides details of a money scam perpetuated by gypsies. Man pops in to call attention to Boy's insensitivity to Gypsies, but replaces the expected word "animals" with "Gypsies" (*3CP* 485) in doing so, which is also insensitive. More banter of questionable sensitivity follows the suggestion that maybe Man and Woman are Gypsies come to steal the baby (486, cf. also "dyke" on 467 and "cripples, dwarves" on 490 and "what in the bad old days they used to call mulatto" on 504). To Girl's "Then they're not Gypsies come to steal the baby," Boy backpedals with "What I said was, these people don't *look* like Gypsies—from what I know of how Gypsies look—which may not be much" and "I said that's what Gypsies are *purported* to do." Girl ponders, "Why would anyone want to steal the baby?...To *hurt* us? To injure us beyond salvation?" As Girl leaves to feed the baby, Boy, in a time-conscious (and self-focused rather than baby-focused and therefore unpersuasive) appeal to keep the baby, says to himself:

If there's anybody out there wants to do this to us—to hurt us so…I can take pain and loss and all the rest *later*… But…now? We're *happy*; we love each other; I'm hard all the time; we have a baby. We don't even under*stand* each other yet! (*Pause*) So…give it some thought. Give us some time. (*Pause*) OK? (488)

It's never good when someone says they don't understand someone in an Albee play. Boy will say this to Man, too, in response to Man's announcement that he and Woman have indeed "come to take the baby" (495).

Woman, in a heated exchange with Man, whom she follows onstage, asserts her independent identity with respect to Man and exhibits nostalgia for her youth and accompanying sexuality, relating the tale of a painter who "hanged himself for the love of me" (489). Her parting shot to the painter is also an assertion of identity: "You don't love *me*; you love the *fact* of me." Man expresses disbelief of her story to Woman, to the audience, and to Boy and Girl, applauding the end of her tale and asking Boy and Girl, "Did you like our little performance?" (493) Woman exits with "*false stealth*" and returns with a "*broad wink*" (494-5) to signify the taking of the baby. Man responds with condescension to Boy's shocked "I don't understand" regarding Man's assertion that he and Woman are there to take (have taken?) the baby. Woman says, "You're not being nice"—and later "Well, *that* may be" (513, also said by Man on 504)—which recalls oft-used phrases from *Listening*. To Girl's "WHAT HAVE YOU DONE WITH THE BABY?!" Man and Woman reply, "*[W]hat* baby?"

II. Without Wounds, What Are You? (*3CP* 497-534)

Man enters after the act break and, much like Himself (cf. 166), is abrasive to the audience: "Hurry back in, now; you don't want to miss the exposition," which he suggests "couldn't possibly" have been in the first act, where it traditionally is found. Man later labels, somewhat erroneously, a few depthless facts asserted by Boy as "Exposition" (512), but the speech Man makes at the top of the act before the others return qualifies more as exposition in that it reveals what may be Man's motives for being here. He asserts that "Good things to good people and happy endings" is "fantasy":

> If I saw it *really* happening—all good things to all good people?—would I turn away in horror? Yes, probably: because it could all…stop, could go away, be a single instant of glory, desperately cruel. We can't take glory because it shows us the abyss. That is why we cry at movies—because it's *safe* to; it's all so…beautifully false. (498)

Perhaps Man sees Boy and Girl's happiness as desperately cruel and has enlisted Woman to assist him in addressing the situation. Man says his "sense of what should be rather than what is" "does not apply" and "is an impediment to" "getting through it all," an impediment to facing stark reality, which Man says is based on need. So Man's "We'll see if they let us take the baby from them" (498) follows from wondering "How much they need it" (479).

Reality is also a function of the present moment, highlighted by the reinvention of the end of Act One to begin Act Two. Boy and Girl (and Man and Woman) do again (they do not repeat; cf. *Marriage Play*, 259) what they did before and only make new demands to know where their baby is at the end of the sequence. Woman and Man's new interjections also underscore that the sequence is being done again in the present moment and is not a rote repetition of what came before. As in Act One and in previous Albee plays, honest, passionate distress (Girl's and Boy's here) is condescendingly called "performance" (502). Man re-contextualizes Boy's words and phrases from Act One—"saves time" (507, cf. 477); "great divide" (509; cf. "great declivity," 470); "destination" (510-1; cf. 478, 480)—setting the stage for the reinvention with variants of stories and experiences from Act One, used in a campaign of confusion against Boy and Girl. Man initiates this campaign with the phrase "your real or imagined baby" (503), variations of which will continue until the end of the play. He then says that he has children of a variety of colors, including green, and that he himself has changed colors over time, but then changes "has" to "Had!" children, explaining (and foreshadowing) that *"having* had doesn't mean one *has."* While what Man says seems ludicrous, if he had children that were taken from him, perhaps that has bearing on his qualification for his current task. He says, "I know about children, about who has them…and who does *not"* (505). To complete his preparations, Man introduces the idea of wounds as a condition of adult identity: "Without wounds what *are* you? You're too young for the batterings time brings us" (508) and "If you have no broken heart, how do you know who you are? Have been? Can ever be?" (509)

Albee's interest in the simultaneity of the living/dying process is articulated by Man: "A minute after out-you-slide—or whatever—it's all closing up, closing down, 'til the next time" (509). Boy and Girl's "who *are* you?" (510) to the mysterious Man recalls Sam questioning Elizabeth in *The Lady from Dubuque.* Albee again has someone (Man) say "All Anglo-Saxons are white" (512; cf. Fergus, 224). Woman's interrogation of Girl—"Did you not fake pregnancy" (514)—is perhaps resonant of Honey in *Woolf*.

Man and Woman appropriate Boy's private speech about Girl being his destination to split the couple, Man sharing intimacies with Boy, and Woman sharing intimacies with Girl. Man and Woman then suggest they are Gypsies, Woman recalling the money scam anecdote and suggesting it is Girl's actual experience: "You came to me; you brought your life savings in a paper bag" (511). Man and Woman continue to mix imagery and cast doubt and confuse, to invent and reinvent. Man, citing a letter Boy sent, asserts that Boy loves him, not Girl. Woman accuses Girl of faking pregnancy. Man recalls Boy's arm-breaking attackers: "I came up to you, and I undid my fly…and you know what *I* wanted, what *you* wanted" (516). This prompts Girl to offer her breast to Boy as before, Man and Woman briefly noting their touching tableau before renewing their efforts. Woman recasts Boy as her painter, Girl's doubt now increasing. When Man asks "When were you two lovers?" Woman responds, "Oh…last year, last month, last week, on his way to seeing her at the hospital, on his way from seeing her at the hospital—her and the baby. Earlier today." In response to Man's "Tell me about his penis," Girl affects her own reality-change of tactic: "He doesn't have one!" (519)

Man advises Boy and Girl that the most important question is "not who I think I am, but who I cannot be" and to keep in mind "what we cannot do; who we cannot be." This prompts "*signing-like gestures*" from Woman, presumably to signify importance (521, cf. 523). Man cannot be someone who has met Jesus. If he could have been, would he have tried to stop the Crucifixion? Man's "Would He have made me *not*?" resonates with "We'll see if they let us take the baby from them" earlier. Man suggests that even Jesus might question his identity: was the Crucifixion "what he wanted? The proof he needed?" (523)

Back on the attack, Man recasts himself as Girl in Boy's story of his meeting her and following her to the hospital over protests from Boy and Girl. Man exacerbates the confusion by merging "when we *met*" at the hospital with "When we went to have the baby!" When Boy tells the story of the birth (which was symbolized by a sequence of offstage sound effects at the beginning of the play), Man, Woman, and Girl all remember the pain, Girl showing "*no emotion...merely howling*," Man and Woman disturbingly ecstatic over the memory of blood. Woman and Man suggest it was a movie to cast doubt. Man recalls the money scam but "with the baby in a big paper bag," implying that Girl took her baby to a Gypsy in this fashion, over Girl's protests, which prompt Boy's comfort and Man's announcement of his final tactic, "the old blanket trick," which blanket Woman goes off to retrieve.

Boy again says, "I can take pain and loss and all the rest *later*;... Not now....give us some time" (529, cf. 488). "*After long pause*," Man says, "Time's up," a phrase said again four times before Man decides to "deal finally, once and for all, with the baby," which is revealed not to be in the blanket upon Woman's return. Man and Woman initiate a verbal ritual through which, in three sequences of four measures each, Girl and finally Boy, prepped to change their reality by the act-long antics of Man and Woman, decide they have no baby. In the first sequence (530-1), the simple pattern is broken when Girl does not answer Man's "You have a baby?" In the second, more erratic, sequence (531-3) Man continues to ask his question, Boy urging Girl to "Tell him." Girl says, "I don't know," then is silent, then says, "No; I don't think so," which prompts four responses from Boy and four more denials from Girl before Woman changes Man's "you have a baby?" to "You have no baby" to initiate the close of the second sequence. In the third sequence (533), each measure has Woman then Man then Girl saying "No," and Boy's struggle and decision is characterized by four simple responses—"(*Sobbing*) Yes" then "Yes" then "No?" then "(*Pause*) No"—his last response prompting the coda: Man's "Well then; we're done" and Woman's final "Yes."

Man says again as he and Woman prepare to leave, "Wounds, children, wounds. Learn from it. Without wounds, what are you? If you don't have a broken heart…." After two feeble attempts at renewed resistance— "No baby?" and "I hear it crying!"—denied by Girl, Boy says in defeat, "No baby." Echoing Boy's earlier appeals to keep the baby, Girl says, "No. Maybe later? When we're older…when we can take…terrible things happening? Not now." Boy says again, "I hear it crying," and Girl, in remembrance now rather than denial, says, "I hear it too. I hear it crying too." Unlike earlier in the play ("*baby crying*" on 461-2 and 487), there is no stage direction that calls for sound.

Citing Girl's lactation, Albee assured his biographer that the baby is real but that Boy and Girl "realize they cannot take the pain and loss of having a baby, so it ceases to be real" (Gussow 398). For Boy and Girl, the memory of having the baby is less painful than having and fearing the loss of the baby. Shown the abyss of potentially losing the baby, they can't take the glory of having the baby. Albee told Stephen Bottoms, "Eventually the young couple realize that they *cannot have* the baby, and therefore it must disappear" and that the baby is "A reality first, and then an absence. A real baby that is taken away" (*SMM* 289). Did the baby disappear, or was it taken away? If taken away, Woman secures the baby long before the end of the play, so where is the baby during that time? Who is taking care of the baby? Do Man and Woman have offstage accomplices, perhaps someone from *The American Dream*'s Bye Bye Adoption Service? And what are the consequences for the baby? Will the baby survive abandonment as Woman survived abandonment by her husband (472)? Or, like the painter Woman abandoned in her youth (493), will the baby die because it cannot cope with what it has lost? Loss and its accompanying wounds are associated with reality and identity in this play. One of the things Man knows about children is the "color of loss" (505). The loss of their child, especially because it is effected by the reality of their need, is a wound that will shape the young couple's identities throughout their marriage. While animal nature is not a key concern of this play, Woman says she belongs with "the healthy animals" (492), and Man considers animal babies in his definition of "What is a baby?" (509)

Albee's usual linguistic playfulness and precision reflect this play's concern with memory and time. After Girl says "you can't remember pain," she then asserts that giving birth hurt "As I remember" (461). Man concludes that "not being remembered" and "being forgotten" are "not quite" the same thing (467). The characters often qualify their statements, often to be more precise about time. Woman says, "That's the first thing I want you to know—well, the second actually, the first being...having been . . ." (472). Boy says of Girl in the hospital, "I assumed you weren't—wouldn't be" dead (482). Boy makes several qualifications that break up the flow of the prelude to his broken-arm remembrance, an event that occurred after "the Hopeless Mothers gig" at a "Mother's Milk" benefit (462-4). Boy waxes "hyperbolic" about his exploration of Girl's body (470-1). Woman, speaking of her breasts, makes a significant qualification: "Didn't you want to suck them? Everyone else did...wanted to" (517). Man says, "'That's they' doesn't sound right, though it is" (474). When Woman was little she used to say "needles" for needless, dropping the word's final letter. A phrase with first letters transposed appears again: "wangled teb" (491, 534; cf. 293). Man willfully misinterprets "her baby" (502-3) and "baby doctor"

(526); says, "Goodness, I'm saying 'good' a lot"; riffs on a word origin; calls for precision (507); and says he's always liked the poetic "ope" for open (510). Man says the envoy with gifts of silk speaks in "his silkiest tone," prompting appreciative chuckles from Woman, for which he thanks her (520). Finally, Albee can't resist having Man say in praise of Christ's Sermon on the Mount speech, the one with infinite loaves and fishes, "One could dine out on that…*forever!*" (523)

This play features the most speeches delivered to the audience, including several long monologues, since *The Man Who Had Three Arms*. In a speech that makes assertions about the relative frequencies of attendance of blind and deaf audience members, Man notes that most plays come at you "by the ear" (479). The second act of the play begins with Man's discussion of intermission and a ritual restaging of the end of the first act by all the characters; Woman's assertion that she is "not an actress" (472) underlines the fact that the characters are not acting but rather doing again what they did before. Albee makes characteristic allowances in his directions here, too: Man is permitted to "*improvise briefly*" (466), and Girl appears "*as naked as the actress will allow*" (471). Boy understands neither Man's stage command to "Hold!" nor Woman's qualification that the command's origins are Elizabethan. Albee uses stage directions to guide the sequences and measures of the play's ritual ending: "*Don't rush this section*," "*increased tempo here*," "*varying intensities and tempi*," "*Response tempi easy now*" (530-3). Again, Albee has abstractly-named, paired characters in a sparse environment, the placement of the chairs here (461) resonant with that of *The American Dream* (*1CP* 98), another play in which parents are not suited to have a baby. Although the play ends in a climactic ritual, its structure is dependent upon its recurrent imagery and its central themes of identity shaped by loss and reality shaped by time and need, making this play, like the last three, hard to characterize as either climactic or episodic.

THE GOAT, OR WHO IS SYLVIA?

The Goat, or
Who Is Sylvia?

How do we face the stark reality of a situation that is "Beyond all the rules" (*3CP* 611) of our experience? In this play, subtitled *(Notes Toward a Definition of Tragedy)*, Albee gives us a situation that requires us to question our unconscious acceptance of societal mores, the radical breach of which provides an opportunity for self-scrutiny. Resonant with tragic form, the first scene presents a moral problem; the second scene laments the reversals of fortune associated with the moral breach; and in the third scene the inevitable consequences of the moral choice are effected. Albee's "notes" suggest that the isolation effected by the impossibility of anyone understanding our flawed and irreversible action is as definitively tragic as the fate that compelled the action.

I. Who Is Sylvia? (*3CP* 539-570)

The willful misinterpretation of questions, insistence on precision, and complimentary impulses (even in moments of extreme stress) that characterize Albee's couples are especially evident in Stevie and Martin, perhaps Albee's happiest couple, which makes their dissolution even more upsetting. Martin's struggle with his memory and Stevie's suggestion "that everything going right is a sure sign that everything's going wrong, of all the awful to come" (glory showing us the abyss) resonate with concerns in *The Play About the Baby*, and Martin's wondering whether his "mind's going" resonates with Agnes in the opening of *A Delicate Balance* (Zinman also notes a resonance in Martin's challenging Ross about friendship rights, 556; cf. Zinman 150). The "awful to come" is foreshadowed by Stevie's questions: "Where have you been?" "Does she smell funny?" "Something's going on, isn't it!?" "Who is Sylvia?" Martin answers, "Sylvia is a goat!" and then breaks the jesting sequence to say again in a normal tone, "She's a goat," but the notion is unbelievable and therefore dismissed by Stevie as a joke until she receives Ross's letter of proof. Ross's introduction of Martin for the program he is filming concerns Martin's architectural accomplishments but also foreshadows the "awful to come" with respect to Martin's family: "[S]ome people matter in extraordinary ways, in ways which affect the lives of the rest of us." Ross's "You're at the…pinnacle of your success" and Martin's "You mean it's all downhill from here?" foreshadow Martin's reversal of fortune upon the discovery of his action.

Ross opposes Martin's continued actions with Sylvia and so could be called Martin's antagonist, and Ross also champions offensive-but-widely-tolerated assumptions and phrases that we are prompted to rethink when Martin's extreme breach of moral decorum gives us occasion to take a meta-view of our moral assumptions. Ross characterizes

Martin's son Billy's homosexuality as a "phase." He is a snob about his film crew. He equates the phrases "in love" and "Ficky-fack!" He uses the phrases "a couple of bimbos" and "big tits." Martin's attempts to confide in Ross about his profound experience of meeting Sylvia are met with Ross's assumptions of human lust or love on Martin's part. Martin frequently says, "You don't understand," a recurring concern of Albee's characters. Upon being shown a photograph, Ross confirms, "This is Sylvia…who you're fucking." Martin's "Whom" in this tense context is a less consequential expression of the same compulsive nature which has led him into a relationship with a goat.

II. You Have Brought Me Down (*3CP* 571-605)

After receiving Ross's letter, Stevie demands, with four repetitions of "let us not pretend" (573), that Martin confront the reality of Ross's action and the subsequent necessity of Martin articulating his own action. But Stevie is resistant to accepting the reality of what Martin has done. She says, "[K]nowing it's true is one thing, but *believing* what you *know*…well, there's the tough part" (580), and her demand to know what Martin has to say is accompanied by a plea: "Make me not *believe* it! Please, make me *not believe* it" (583). Stevie resists both because Martin's action is inconceivable and because it has identity- and reality-changing consequences for her; Martin's tragic reversal of fortune, his fall, is also Stevie's. Stevie says, "I *fell* in love with you? No…I rose into love with you" (594), but compares her realization of what Martin has done, her tragic recognition, to the experience of falling off a building (580). She asks, "Martin, did you ever think you'd come back from your splendid life, walk into your living room and find you had no life left?" (582) She prompts Martin to continue his story with "Destroy me" (586) and with sacrificial imagery: "I'm naked on the table; take all your knives! Cut me! Scar me forever!" (595) When Martin equates his love of Stevie with his love of Sylvia, Stevie "*howls three times*" (599, confer Lear's five howls) in resistance to facing an undesired reality. Resonant with both the fate and the flaws of tragic protagonists and with the irretrievable consequences of tragic actions, Martin characterizes his union with Sylvia as destined, realizing (as opposed to deciding) "that she and I were going to go to bed together," "That what could not happen was *going* to" (601). Stevie characterizes Martin and herself as reality-facing people—"we see what's hideously wrong in what most people accept as normal"—experiencing a reality that can't be faced because Martin "screwed *up*!" He's "broken something and it can't be fixed!" She exclaims "*I* am destroyed" and "You have brought me down, and, Christ!, I'll bring you down with me!" (604-5), these words and her destruction of Martin's other love resonant with Medea's poisoning of Glauce.

In pausing to acknowledge shared tastes, appreciate witticisms, and insist on precision, Stevie and Martin effect a momentary detachment from the life-altering reality they are experiencing. Martin agrees with Stevie's judgment of Ross's letter as flowery (573) and comments positively on the eloquence of both his wife and son (576-7). Stevie pretends to puzzle the meaning of "haberdasher," prompting a response from Martin (581-2). They each reward witticisms with "Very good, by the way" (584, 595). Martin corrects Stevie's characterization of Sylvia as bleating with "That's sheep" (603). Stevie also breaks or overturns objects nine times (586-603): visceral, irrational actions effected to cope with the irrational reality she is having to face.

Albee said he wanted audiences of *The Goat* to "imagine themselves in the situation, and really think hard about how they would respond if it was happening to them" (*SMM* 284), but he is also putting us in a place of moral detachment so that we can ask ourselves why some things are morally inconceivable and some are not. The crass expectation of infidelity Martin describes (593) should be inconceivable. Stevie chastises ("You men are the end") Martin's reference to his new assistant as "Lucy something" just after she refers to the same assistant as "the one with the hooters" (579). Martin's calling his son Billy a "fucking faggot" should be inconceivable "because he's not that kind of man. He's a decent, liberal, right-thinking, talented, famous, gentle man" (572), but after this Martin still makes judgmental assumptions about Billy: "go to one of your public urinals, or one of those death clubs" (576). Stevie exhibits touches of homophobic disdain, too. She casually uses "dyke" (581), supposes she should be grateful Sylvia isn't male (585), and makes the horrific accusation "You'll be fucking Billy next" (601). Stevie's unreasonable linkage of one thing she considers immoral (bestiality) with another (homosexuality and/or incest) calls attention to the arch-conservative fallacy that legalizing same-sex marriage will lead to legal pedophilia and bestiality, an association which should be inconceivable but was made as recently as 2016 in the U.S. presidential campaign by Ben Carson. Why aren't the circumstances of a twelve-year-old being continually raped by her father and brother, "one watching the other" (591), as inconceivable as the bestiality those acts led her to?

Stevie insists on making hierarchical (and grammatical) distinctions between human and animal—"Stop calling it *her*!" "*What!* Not *whom*!" (585, 586)—whereas Martin insists on equality. Martin speaks of Sylvia's pure, trusting, innocent, guileless expression (597) and of her soul. Martin counter's Stevie's "It is about fucking! It is about you being an animal!" with "I thought we *all* were…animals" (602). Stevie challenges, "You take advantage of this…creature? You…*rape* this…

animal and convince yourself that it has to do with love!?" (603) Sylvia indeed has no power to characterize this situation. In Shakespeare's *The Two Gentlemen of Verona*, from which the song "Who is Sylvia?" originates (cited by Stevie, 584), Sylvia was almost raped by Proteus, but she would not have had the power to label and redress that crime had it occurred.

Our inability to understand one another has been a signature concern of Albee's since his first play. Here Stevie says, "You love me? I don't understand….How can you love me when you love so much less?" (575) Martin "didn't understand" why the people in therapy for their relationships with animals were so unhappy and presumably hopes that upon hearing his explanation Stevie will understand him: "maybe when I've finished you…just listen, please" (589). Martin says "don't you see the 'thing' that happened to me? What nobody under-stands? Why I can't feel what I'm supposed to!? Because it relates to nothing? It can't have happened! It did, but it *can't* have!" and speaks of "an understanding so intense, so natural" that he has with Sylvia (598). In reference to Martin's sexual activity with both herself and a goat, Stevie is aghast that Martin can "do these two things…and not understand how it…cannot be dealt with—how stop and forgiveness have nothing to do with it…How stopping has nothing to do with having started" (604-5). She promises Martin that she will bring him down with her and leaves the house.

III. What Cannot Be Undone (*3CP* 605-622)

In response to Billy's confusion, Martin says, "You don't know who I *am* anymore.…Well…neither does your mother" (608), which implies that Martin does know who he is, but Martin has to be shocked into facing reality by Ross:

> MARTIN: Yes; all right, it *was* sick, and yes, it *was* compulsive, and . . .
>
> ROSS: IS! Not was! IS!
>
> MARTIN: (*Stopped in his tracks*) I...I . . .
>
> ROSS: IS!
>
> MARTIN: (*Gathering himself*): Is. All right. *Is. Is* sick; *is* compulsive. (619)

Even after this concession, though, Martin wants to believe he is in control of himself and wants to share blame for his fall with Ross: "I could have handled it! You didn't have to bring it all down!" (619) Martin knows that the inconceivability of his experience has isolated him, but he still longs for someone to at least understand the isolation if not the experience: "Why can't anyone understand this...that I am *alone*." To Martin's "You *do* understand; *don't* you" Ross says, "No" (621).

While he has us considering the inconceivable, Albee presents us with two situations that highlight how distinctions between love and sex can get confused and suggests that momentary involuntary responses are not always fraught with meaning and moral consequence. Billy, simultaneously grateful for his parents and grieving over the consequences that Martin's actions have caused the family, expresses his love and despair by hugging and kissing Martin, which leads to Billy kissing Martin on the mouth as Ross enters unseen. Martin breaks from the kiss but continues to comfort Billy. Martin counters Ross's disdain with "This boy is hurt! I've hurt him, and he still loves me! You fucker! He loves his father, and if it...clicks over and becomes—what?—sexual for...just a moment...so what!?" Billy realizes "It *did*. It clicked over, and you were just another...man. I get confused...sex and love." Ross, wanting to link Martin's bestiality with this moment, retorts, "Jesus! Sick! What is it...contagious?" (616)

Further illustrating his point, Martin relates the experience of a man whose "baby in his lap was making him hard—not arousing him; it wasn't sexual, but it was happening." Then "the moment passed, and he knew it had all been an accident, that it meant...nothing—that nothing was connected to anything else" (617). Ross's "Is there anything you people don't get off on?" prompts Martin's diatribe on moral hypocrisy that brings to mind Julian's recounting of his fantasies before succumbing to (Miss) Alice:

> Is there anything anyone doesn't get off on, whether we admit it or not—whether we know it or not? Remember Saint Sebastian with all the arrows shot into him? He probably came! God knows the faithful did! Shall I go on!? You want to hear about the cross!? (618)

Martin, upon discovering that Ross's motives for exposing him to Stevie are practical rather than moral, exclaims, "I can do whatever I want, and that's what matters!? That people will find *out*!? Fuck the...thing *itself*!? Fuck what it *means*!?...I thought it had to do with love and loss, and it's only about...getting *by*" (620).

Martin's actions are tragic in part because they are fated to bring about irretrievable consequences. He has done "what cannot be undone" (610). Martin is beyond hope, and his situation is "Beyond all the rules" (611). Martin says, "I am diminished" (613). Billy says that Martin is "digging a pit so deep...we'll all fall in" and never be able to climb out again (614). The fate of Martin's family is irrevocably intertwined with his own, a situation resonant with that of Oedipus, who after he blinds himself pleads with his daughters to accept the stark reality of how his actions will affect their lives. Resonant with the sacrificial imagery associated with ancient tragedy, Stevie, covered in blood, returns with the goat that she has killed, with Sylvia, whose death Stevie asserts was fated: "Why are you surprised? What did you expect me to do?" Martin's protests of Sylvia's innocence are met with Stevie's sentencing of them both: "She loved you...you say. As much as *I* do" (621-2).

Early in the play, Stevie attempts to bring a distracted Martin back to himself by asking him to identify himself with her: "Who *am* I? Who am *I*?" (542) And Martin's actions with respect to Sylvia irreparably strain the bonds of his marriage and family, because Stevie and Billy now see Martin and themselves differently as a consequence of those actions: their identities have been shaped by his reality-changing actions. Stevie asks Martin how he "can do these two things...and not understand...how *I* am destroyed? How *you* are? How I cannot admit it though I *know* it!? How I cannot deny it because I cannot *admit* it!?" (604) Billy's confidence in his father's identity is damaged—"I know who you're supposed to be, but ..." (607)—and he characterizes Martin as digging a pit into which his family has fallen and out of which they cannot climb (614). Billy's description of his "absolutely normal" upbringing (612-4) doesn't qualify him as one of Albee's damaged children, but Zinman suggests that what Billy experiences here may change that (Zinman 150). Billy goats, like humans, have kids, and here Billy twice refers to himself as a kid as well as making reference to giving a speech on his "hind legs" (3*CP* 613). Countering Martin's assertion of a soul connection with Sylvia, Stevie insists that there are distinctions between human and animal and that Martin's relationship "is about you being an animal" immediately before her rage prompts her to make a "*huge animal sound*" (602-3).

Calls for precision with respect to grammar, meaning, and time are here, as well as puns and epigrams. Stevie amends "ranunculus" to "ranunculi" (540). Martin says, "I don't know who she is, as far as I know" (544), and Stevie counters Martin's "Be serious" with "It's too serious for that" (593). "Old man" is a term of endearment, but "old Todd" is odd (548-550). "Dandled" is a lovely word to Martin (550), but Stevie hates "spouses" (581). Martin amends Ross's "who" to "whom" (550), and Billy counters Martin's charge of mixed metaphors with "Semanticist!" (608) Ross says of gay Billy, "He'll straighten out—to make a pun" (551). There are amendments of "was" to "*is*" (554), "*couldn't*" to "*haven't*" (583), "wasn't" to "*isn't*" (585), "wasn't" to "no longer was" (591), "was" to "still is" (in reference to Martin's mother's painting that Stevie has just broken, 595-6), "at" to "on" (596), and Ross's correction of Martin: "IS! Not *was!*" (619) There is banter over linguistic precision (556, 584). Martin's "Are you agreeing?" prompts Stevie to redirect her false politeness: "No. Just get on with it" (590). Finally, there is Stevie's brilliant "Women in deep woe often mix their metaphors" (595).

For only the second time since *Listening*, no one addresses the audience, and this play marks the only time Albee specifically characterizes his work as occurring in "*The present*" (538), although his stage directions frequently call for amendments of the text to reflect the present moment. There are several theatrical references in addition to Shakespeare's "Who is Sylvia?" Martin and Stevie banter in "*greatly exaggerated Noel Coward*" style (546-7); "Large Alice" (563) recalls *Tiny Alice*, another Albee play about the consequences of succumbing to desire; "Oh, Dad!" "Poor Dad?" (574) references an Arthur Kopit play;

Stevie's name said twice and a slammed door recall the end of Ibsen's *A Doll's House*; and reference to the Eumenides (551-2) recalls the ancient tragedy as well as foreshadows Stevie's vengeance. Any definition of tragedy includes how human character is shaped by response to moral dilemmas. Because concepts like Oedipal incest have become intellectual over the years, new taboos or extremes of human behavior must be explored to invoke a response visceral enough to induce catharsis. Albee, in exploring a definition of tragedy, builds upon its classical meaning with additional considerations of moral hypocrisy and of our tragic inability to make ourselves understood or to exist independently of the moral choices of others.

There are minor repetitions of Martin's story to Ross when retold to Stevie and of Stevie's reading of Ross's letter. The strongest sense of ritual accompanies the animal sacrifice at the end of the play, supported verbally by Martin's "I'm sorry," said thrice. There are several intense, eloquent, emotional monologues here from Stevie (580-1, in which Albee's concerns with dying and disengagement recur; 594; 604-5) and Billy (613-4). Albee grounds his radical subject matter in conservative dramaturgy for this play. His characters have specific names; the environment is a living room, albeit one that Stevie will make reflect the play's destruction and chaos with her broken and overturned objects; and the structure is traditional, progressing linearly within about 24 hours to a climax.

OCCUPANT

Occupant

The life of Albee's friend, sculptor Louise Nevelson, is the subject of his play about how identity is intuitive and must be pursued and how the reality of that identity is sometimes at odds with the facts. Nevelson says "you got somebody in you right from the start, and if you're lucky you figure out who it is and you *become* it. People who don't *become* are…well, look around you. So don't talk to me about facts" (*3CP* 639). This imagery is resonant of the sculpting process, as is her interviewer Man's chipping away at Nevelson's resistance in order to reveal her. Her assertion above is also resonant of Albee's aversion to closing down, but in the creative process of discovering her identity—"I knew what I wanted; I just didn't know what it was" (673)—Nevelson had long down periods. Consciousness of stark reality—"this awful knowledge that everything's fucked up"—does not always correlate with *facing* stark reality: "if you go numb you can sleepwalk your way through it for a very long time" (672). But Nevelson never gave up on her potential: "if you finally come *into* yourself like I did, if you finally know the space you…occupy…well, then…you go on.…You work harder than ever" (692).

I. You Got Somebody In You Right From The Start (*3CP* 626-664)

Nevelson's interviewer, Man, informs her that "Time passes. You're not as…recognizable now as you were" before her death in 1988. Nevelson ties identity to existence ("You might as well not exist—have existed") and then, countering Man's "Well, sure, if fame is the only thing that matters," ties her identity to her work: "Not fame—recognition of what you've done." Nevelson asserts, "*I* know who I am," and thwarts Man's attempts to pin her down to facts as she recounts the story of her life, which she prefaces with "You don't fit in—so you make everything fit to you." She challenges Man's "I'm after you" with "Yeah? Who's *that*? Who am *I*? I'm a lot of people, honey and I shift all the time." In response to Man's accusation that she occasionally tells "outright lies," she again asks, "Who *am* I?" followed by, "What was my name…when I was born?" forcing Man to acknowledge that she "became Louise Nevelson" and making the point that in order to "become" one must "turn into," which may necessitate occasional conflicts with facts. Nevelson tells of the famous writer (who had also changed his name) who

> NEVELSON:…took me up in his hands and he said to my family that I was destined for greatness—a baby; a little baby.
> MAN: Built for greatness was the way I heard it. Built.

NEVELSON: Built? Destined? So?

MAN: There's a difference, maybe. (641)

Destined is prophetic, while built implies potential. Both character-izations fit. Nevelson says, "I knew I was going to become somebody very special. No...that I *was* somebody very special....but I had no idea what it *was*—what the special *was*—just that it *was*. I had to grow into it, I guess" (640).

Nevelson declares, "I've never wanted anything to *own* me—or *any*one. I've never wanted to *belong* to anything—or any*one*, I guess." Man's prompts lead her to reflections on anti-Semitism in school and her life-changing marriage. Nevelson announces to her audience, "I'll tell it my way...so you'll understand," and relates how dinner with Bernard Nevelson led to marriage with Charles Nevelson before asking, "You, understand, no? A way out...up? We were immigrants; I wasn't even a citizen, and here was this rich Nevelson family decid-ing I belonged with *them*." She chides Man's puzzlement with "Were you around in nineteen-twenty?...an immigrant?...a Jew?...a girl?" Man's answer to all four questions is "no," which prompts Nevelson's "He doesn't *understand* anything." New York was "where I belonged, and I *knew* it," but "You don't own somebody just because you marry them." She says of her role as wife, "I played the game, but...it wasn't me." She was "a rotten mother," "had to go to bed for a year," was "going down," and had "a very, very slow nervous breakdown." When Man asks what kept her from suicide, she says it was her experience at age eleven of a "huge black horse...running, alone, with no harness, or carriage." "Nothing has ever affected me like that. Ever." "It was free." In addition to the importance of understanding and an image of going down(hill), there are other recurring motifs here. Nevelson is tall (645) with a short husband (651-2). She sees someone else in her mirror: "the woman in the mirror looked great, but...who *was* she?" She had a singular experience with a boy at age fifteen. Also, Man makes an abrupt call for an intermission.

II. You Finally Come *Into* Yourself (*3CP* 665-700)

Before Nevelson returns, Man worries again, "You say things enough and people believe them," but before resumption of her life story Nevelson counters, "You gotta be real careful with these types, these 'interviewers.' Especially if you're dead. They take all sorts of liberties" (confer *Fam and Yam*). And indeed Man is not perfect in his objectivity. Nevelson calls him on "adding" the adjective "scary" when quoting from his notes a phrase she used earlier. Nevelson returns to the subject of her son and then her long breakdown, of which she says, "People know something's wrong, but they don't know what, and they don't know how awful the stuff inside is...(*Pokes her chest*) inside *you*! You can go on a very long time and nobody can hear you screaming." This is resonant of Henden's tapping his head and saying "Nobody gets in there with you" (215) and of Martin's lament that no one understands that he is alone. Of Nevelson's trip to Europe that brought her out of her breakdown, Man says, "You were happy." She replies, "No, I wasn't happy. I was alone." Her husband was against her going, citing the mandates of traditional gender roles (675), but her mother understood and funded the trip. Nevelson's reference to her husband as "the little fat bald man" prompts Albee's familiar "You're not nice" (674, cf. 685), and Man and Nevelson exchange "Very good" and "Thank you" in response to Nevelson's "Make your own" speech (673), a paean to self-reliance.

Even though unhappy in Europe, there were oases (as Himself would say, 148): "every once in a while something would happen that would...take me out of myself—take me beyond...*me*." And back in New York she says of seeing Japanese Noh theatre costumes in a museum, "[T]here are things in us we find parallel outside us." "Everything opened up...and I knew, and I said, Oh, my God, life is worth living if civilization can give us this." A turning point like her marriage, seeing the costumes gave her "a whole new life." She was also greatly inspired by the utilitarian art she saw in a museum of African sculpture, but its influence wasn't evident "right away; not for a long time. I'm slow; things get in there and work their way back up." She says that it took twenty-seven years to "become Louise Nevelson" after her return from Europe, "to find out who that 'you' is—what that 'you' is—and...*occupy* that *space*."

She worked throughout those twenty-seven years, experiencing the sexism of critics: "We learned the artist is a woman in time to check our enthusiasm...Had it been otherwise we might have hailed these sculptural expressions as by surely a great figure among moderns." She made sacrifices in her personal life: "You learn after a while that there isn't room for everything." She was lonely "a *lot*, before I figured out who I was." Man responds to her "do you know how tough it was to be an artist and a woman?" with "Even today." Of her hysterectomy, she says, "It was a tumor; women get them; it was fine....They cut my past out." Of her breast reduction surgery she says, "They got in my way."

She began to fill her house with discarded wood and then began to stand it up. "And suddenly there it all was! And I had a show of it... and it was wonderful! It was a whole world! And I looked at it and I started to dance." Resonant with her characterization of the profound experience of seeing the horse as a child, she says, "I never felt more free in my life!" Articulating the fruition of her lifelong awareness of having a special but unknown quality, she says, "All of a sudden I had become *me*, and I was *that!*" Man says she "became a celebrity," was "famous for a long time," and was "rich." This was balanced by a complicated relationship with her son, envious vipers in the art world, and the same depressions as before that "just became more… tolerable." Eventually Nevelson, an incessant smoker, developed lung cancer. Using a familiar Albee phrase, she says she "went downhill pretty quick." In the hospital, she had them take her name off her door and replace it with "Occupant." Of the rumor that her nurse tied her big toes together in "some primitive ritual" after her death, she says, echoing a major concern of the play, "People will say anything." Man ends the play exactly as he began it: "Ladies and Gentlemen…the great American sculptor…Louise Nevelson."

Occupant is primarily about Nevelson's pursuit of a special identity which she intuited as a child but which required the creative processes of her life and work to discover and occupy. It also calls attention to the murky relationship between reality and truth, the unintentional discrepancy between what's "*really* true and what is embroidery, or what's just slightly misremembered," and the calculation of downright lies "made up for a reason—to disprove a fact, or…make everything just a little…ambiguous" (665). Nevelson's bonds and conflicts with her mother and father, her husband, and her son are discussed, Nevelson more absent and damaged than her child in this case. Although there is no discussion of animal nature, Nevelson's experience of the horse as a child was one of the most affecting of her life.

Nevelson questions phrases and clichés throughout the play, saying, "Is that what they say…none taken?" (627) and of "tough row to hoe":

"what does it mean? What tough row?" (634). There are signature corrections of tense or meaning: "do" to "did" (twice, 628), "not exist" to "have existed" (629), and "Couldn't, not wouldn't" (635). Man, like Martin, notes the mixing of metaphors (689). Many of the speeches are delivered "out" to the audience, and the interplay between speeches made "out" then "in" or vice-versa can be humorous or otherwise dramatically effective, as they were in *The Play About the Baby*. There is attention to theatrical convention—canned applause (626) and an announcement of intermission (664)—and Albee's usual attention to the present moment: changing the year of the play and the time since Nevelson's death to "*whatever it is*" and "*whatever is correct*" (629), respectively, and attending to potential audience response (679, 692). There are theatrical references to Tennessee Williams (Blanche, 638) and even to a musical: Man exclaims after Nevelson's reference to singing in the Austrian mountains, "The hills were alive with the sound of music!" (678)

There is little sense of ritual or repetition of text here, but the play is bookended with repetitive announcements like Jerry's story, *Ballad*, and *Fragments*. Nevelson usually doesn't get far without being prompted by Man, and her extended passages are reserved for moments of great significance in her life, the longest being her discovery of wood. Man's treatise on truth at the top of the second act is actually one of the longer uninterrupted passages. The interview of Nevelson, who looks "*much like the later photographs*" (625), yields fewer monologues than the lecture of *The Man Who Had Three Arms*. Albee uses another simple, open environment for this play: platforms and the eventual revelation of Nevelson's sculpture at the edges (625). Nevelson's enclosure for the opening and closing of the play is described as a costume "*cage*," then "*the cage, or shell*" (626), and finally as a "*carapace*" (700). Like the four plays that preceded *The Goat*, *Occupant* is somewhat climactic in form but spans a lifetime and is dominated by its central idea of identity being an intuitive and creative pursuit.

Occupant is Albee's first published play to feature text written by him for a character named after a non-fictional person. Bessie Smith did not appear in her play. Mao's words were his own. *The Lorca Play* remains unpublished, though Albee intended to include it in a fourth volume of his collected plays (*3CP* 7). *I Look Back Now on Andre Gide*, which Albee said was not about Andre Gide (Wallach) and which was not mentioned in the list of plays being considered for the fourth volume, was pulled two months before its slated Off-Broadway opening and replaced with *Occupant* (Lefkowitz).

KNOCK! KNOCK! WHO'S THERE!?

Pages   Outline

(*3CP*)

I. Is Anyone There?

704   A. Help!

704   B. Hello?

704   C. Let me out!

.

.

.

N. Is Anyone There?

704   A. Help!

704   B. Hello?

704   C. Let me out!

where N = minutes "theatre is accessible to patrons" (702)/minutes of one iteration of the text

Knock! Knock! Who's There!?

K *nock! Knock! Who's There!?*, the "one-page additional frippery" (*3CP* 7) that closes the third volume of Albee's collected plays, might be asking us to reflect upon established traditions, or it might just be a joke. As opposed to a standard joke, the knock-knock joke invites the verbal participation of the listener. Perhaps this play reminds us that audience members can make their own critical assessments of a production. Or it could remind us that the responsibility of the critic should not be taken for granted, that the critical function has great potential if executed well.

I. Is Anyone There? (*3CP* 704)

The text is a 30-second persuasive appeal. The critic attempts to gain attention with emphatic knocks and shouts for help. The critic then attempts to hold the attention of any audience he may have gained beyond the boarded-up door to make a persuasive case. First the problem is stated: "Someone's locked me in here!" Then the desired solution: "Let me out!" Then the justification: "I have to be at the performance! I'm a critic!" Finally, the critic checks the attentiveness of the potential audience—"Is there anyone there? (*Pause*) Help?"—before summarizing ("I'm a critic!") and making an emphatic call for action: "Let me out! (*Knock. Knock*) Help! (*Pause*) Help!" The final stage direction is "*Repeat endlessly.*"

N. Is Anyone There? (*3CP* 704)

Albee says that "The entire play should be performed over and over again whenever the theatre is accessible to the patrons" and that "[t]he words, as opposed to the knock-knocks, are recorded, of course, and come from a speaker behind the door, I would imagine" (702). If a person is not required to speak behind the door for hours, then presumably a person is not required to knock behind the door for hours, although "Ideally, if we were to touch the door, we would feel the thumping" (702). Should a mechanical knocker be devised and programmed to sync with the voice recording? Should knocking be done in rotating shifts by theatre staff and crews? Presumably, the final stage direction, "*repeat endlessly,*" means that a 30-second recording of the "entire play" is looped, or does "performed over and over again" allow for a longer recording of the text being done again ritualistically rather than simply repeating a single iteration in a 30-second loop? We "come upon this play by accident" "walking somewhere in the theatre." Do we know it's a looped recording and view the play as akin to an art installation, or do we think it's real at first, maybe even trying to help before we get the joke? There are none of Albee's usual stage directions to account for potential audience response to questions, because the voice is recorded and unable to respond. Perhaps we are to call into question the unwritten rule "I have to be at the performance! I'm a critic!" Perhaps Albee is asking us to consider the contradiction between our desire for the critical function and what critics offer us. Perhaps we're being asked to consider why we allow critics to shape the reality of what we think about plays if we wouldn't, in stark reality, help a critic who was trapped.

In the play, it is essential to the critic's identity to attend the performance, and there seems to be an air of panic about the loss that will accompany failure to meet the responsibilities attendant upon that identity. Or is it just animal panic from being trapped? Are we being asked to consider the assumptions that shape the reality of our theatre experience? Does the critic have to be at the performance? Can a play occur offstage without live actors?

The unnamed critic in the text hopes there is an audience beyond the door and speaks as if there is one. There is also an awareness of an impending performance and an assumption of the necessity of the critical function to theatrical performance. Even in a single iteration, a sense of ritual can be achieved by the circular structure of the text: repetitions of "*Knock*" (22 times, the first 7 followed by exclamation points), "*Pause*" (6 times), "Help" (8 exclamations, 1 declaration, 1 interrogation), "Hello?" (3 times), "Is anyone there?" and "Is there anyone there?," "Let me out!" (twice), and "I'm a critic!" (twice). The only text not repeated is "Someone's locked me in here!" and "I have to be at the performance!" and "*Repeat endlessly*." That accounts for all 74 words. The environment is a doorway, boarded up hastily and imperfectly and behind which the critic is confined, that we come upon by accident walking somewhere in the theatre (702).

AT HOME AT THE ZOO

At Home at the Zoo

Nearly fifty years after introducing us to Peter, Albee decides to take us into Peter's home and introduce us to Peter's wife, Ann, as well in *Homelife*, Act One of *At Home at the Zoo*, of which *The Zoo Story* is Act Two. The pairing of these plays highlights a signature concern of Albee's: the dichotomy between our animal natures and our civilizing impulses, our circumspection. Because our animal desires come with a price, we seek the safety of circumspection, an objective distance or meta-awareness that leads us to phrases like Ann's "thinking about thinking about it" (*AHZ* 9) and "what I can't imagine—but I imagine imagining" (24). But indulging our specific, subjective animal needs leads us into conflicts physical or emotional or into isolation: others cannot completely fulfill our desires; we talk hoping for at least an understanding, but that rarely occurs. Ann says "that I know you love me—as you understand it, and I'm grateful for that—but not enough, that you don't love me the way I need it, or I think I do; that that's not in your makeup—not *in* you, perhaps, or that maybe there's no one could do it, could love me as much as I *need* to be loved" (19-20). Ann entices Peter into an imagination of animal chaos that quickly fades; Jerry, upon enticing Peter into actual chaos, says, "[I]t's all right, you're an animal. You're an animal, too" (46).

I. Homelife (*AHZ* 5-26)

Just as he was—and will be—in *The Zoo Story*, Peter is entranced in his reading when someone attempts to get his attention. Jerry says, "I've been to the zoo," (27) until Peter attends, asking, "Do you mind if we talk?" (28) shortly thereafter. Ann does not need a preliminary I've-been-to-the-kitchen sequence and simply asserts, "We should talk." Unlike Jerry, she leaves until Peter realizes she was talking to him and calls her back. Peter amends "deepening" to "deepened" and "off" to "out" and "falling" to "slipping" (5-8; cf. "north" to "northerly," 27). Peter's distraction is not specific to this day with Ann and Jerry; Ann relates another occasion on which "you never heard me." Ann's reference to "microwaves" and Albee's amendment of Peter's salary to "two hundred thousand a year" (30) keep us from setting the play in 1958, when *The Zoo Story* was written, but Ann (like Woman 4 in *Fragments*, *3CP* 446) still says "icebox" (*AHZ* 19). Ann persists in getting Peter to talk; Jerry persists in getting Peter to listen. Ann, like Jerry, calls out Peter's falseness: "This is your party thing; this Trollope thing; you do this at parties" (8). Peter's disparagement of Trollope's autobiography seems a better fate than Trollope's never being heard of in the lament of *Mao*'s Long-Winded Lady (*2CP* 296).

Ann refers to Peter as "Mr. Circumspection," implying that he is wary or unwilling to take risks sexually, in a sequence of the play (*AHZ*

8-16) that considers circumcision and other cuts as circumspect. The original meaning of circumspection was to look around, which resonates with some meta-awareness and ambiguity—"Either; both" (9, 12; cf. "Yes…no," 24)—in this sequence. Ann says she "was thinking about thinking about" "having my breasts cut off" (cf. Nevelson, *3CP* 694) as a means of avoiding breast cancer. Peter resists the idea and perks up at Ann's change of topic, which Ann notices: "why are we moving this conversation away from me." Peter believes that his "circumcision is going away," that his "penis seems to be…retreating." This leads to a discussion about the appropriate timing and permissions necessary for circumcision. Ann notes that "Circumcising the girls" in Africa doesn't happen until puberty and is a means of sexual circumspection: "Kills all the sensation—all the pleasure, when they're old enough for pleasure. Cuts down on the infidelity."

Like Jack and Gillian in *Marriage Play*, Peter and Ann struggle with communicating subjective identity and with the contradiction between desire and what a spouse can offer. Ann says, "I'm not a generality; I'm a *person*" and "you don't love me the way I need it" (*AHZ* 18, 19). Echoing Jack in *Marriage Play*, she says, "nothing is…ultimately…sufficient—not you, not us, not…me" (*AHZ* 20, cf. *3CP* 302-3). Ann also goes out and comes back in like Jack (*AHZ* 17). Just as Nancy thwarts Charlie in *Seascape*, Ann discourages Peter's tendency to close down. Ann asks Peter what he would "imagine was terrible enough" to wake up and talk to her about in the middle of the night. She chides Peter's resistance to the topic with "we don't *have* [terrible things], *do* we?" His "we're probably going to, one day" (18) foreshadows *The Zoo Story*. Like Charlie, Peter says, "it's not a bad life we've made together" (19). Ann counters Peter's description of marriage as "a smooth voyage on a safe ship" with "we'll never die.…we'll just vanish" (20).

Like *Counting the Ways*, *Homelife* is concerned with animal instincts beneath the veneer of civilization. Ann asserts that Peter is very good "at making love" but is "lousy at fucking," noting, "There are people rise to that—sink to it, if you like—*rise* to that, become animals." "We're animals! Why don't we behave like that...like beasts?! Is it that we love each other too safely, maybe? That we're secure? That we're too...civilized?" (21) Peter shares an event from his past in which he hurt someone that bears upon his reluctance to sexual aggression. Ann says that she wasn't asking for pain, she was "talking about being an animal—nothing more," and that we can have our animal nature "bred out of us—learned away." "It's not pain I want, or loss; it's what I can't imagine—but I imagine imagining" (24). Ann prompts Peter to imagine "a little...disorder around here, a little...chaos" (25), but their mutual fantasy dissipates back into reality with Ann's "We eat ourselves—all up." As in *Fragments*, intimate communication reverts back to polite distance with Ann's cliché "Don't take any wooden nickels" (26). Peter then leaves to go to the park and read.

II. The Zoo Story (*AHZ* 27-47)

The Zoo Story was analyzed above, but I'll make a few notes here about moments that resonate with *Homelife*. Jerry identifies Peter as a dog person and opines that cats "can't be your idea" (29; cf. Peter's "I want a dog" and Ann's "*No* you don't," 7). Jerry's fantasy of Peter's parakeets matches Ann's fantasy of chaos: "you could set them loose in the house and the cats could eat them and die, maybe" (29, cf. 25). Another signal that Jerry is an agent of chaos is when he chides Peter, "What are you trying to do? Make sense out of things? Bring order?" (31) Jerry is less prone to intellectual distancing than Ann and Peter. He lightly mocks Peter, shocked at Jerry's description of his landlady, with "It's for reading about, isn't it?" (35) Ann's slap inspires imagined chaos (25-6); Jerry's punches inspire actual chaos (42-7). Ann's "you don't love me the way I need it" (19) is echoed in Jerry's "Don't you have any idea, not even the slightest, what other people *need*?" (44) Ann says that we can have the reality of "being an animal…bred out of us—learned away" (24). One of the last things Jerry says to Peter is "it's all right, you're an animal. You're an animal, too" (46).

Will Peter's experiences in the park with Jerry affect his and Ann's ability to reach each other? When Ann suggests that she and Peter don't have anything "terrible enough" to merit talking about in the middle of the night, Peter says, "we're probably going to, one day." Ann says "And we may even talk about it" (18). Peter says of his experience at the sex party in college, "There are things you don't say if they don't have anything to do with anything that's ever going to happen again" (24). Surely the visceral immediacy of Jerry's death after impaling himself on the knife he gave to Peter will compel Peter to confide in Ann. Surely Peter won't bury that trauma because "it's for reading about" and not appropriate for civilized discourse.

At Home at the Zoo documents our struggles to face the reality of—to be more at home with—our animal natures. Peter has distanced himself from his animal identity ("I'm not like that," 21); Ann longs to express hers ("Why don't we behave like that…like beasts?!" 21); and Jerry laments our enforced separation: "everyone separated by bars from everyone else, the animals for the most part from each other, and always the people from the animals. But, if it's a zoo, that's the way it is" (42). Animal nature is not just about sex and violence; it is also about the need to bond. Both Ann and Jerry need to talk, to make intimate contact through conversation free of intellectual distancing. Intimacy is as valid a gateway as aggression to get us through the veneer of civilization and closer to our animal instincts.

Ann and Peter challenge or call attention to the meanings of figures of speech: "fly-by-night" (8), "bouncing baby boy" (15-16), "gather my wits about me" (18), "the small hours" (18), and the young people's term "*do* it" (21). Ann says of herself, "she said ironically," (8) and amends Peter's "hacking off" to "*Having* them hacked off" (11). Like other Albee couples, Ann and Peter admire each other's wit: Peter says, "very good" (22), and Ann says, "Touche" (24). There is no meta-awareness of theatre in this play, but Albee asks in his stage directions that we "*Don't rush*" (26) the end of *Homelife* and calls for a "*Tableau*" (46) at the climactic moment of *The Zoo Story*. Jerry has a moment of meta-awareness in that "*for the most part he seems removed from his dying*" (46). While not as ritualistic as other Albee plays, *Homelife* begins with "We should talk" (5) and comes "Full circle" (16) at the midpoint of the play when the opening moment is recalled by Peter. In *The Zoo Story*, Jerry keeps Peter's attention with frequent promises to reveal why he went to the zoo. *At Home at the Zoo* moves from the closed environment of a living room, where our animal natures are perhaps more likely to be caged, to the open environment of a park. While both acts of the play build to a climax, both acts are also centered on the themes of our animal natures dampened by the veneer of civilization and our inability to meet or even understand each other's needs.

ME, MYSELF & I

Me, Myself & I

*M*e, *Myself & I* is Albee's most farcical play since *The American Dream,* that play also being the only other one to explore a special relationship between twins (no offense to the Rainey twins in *Ballad).* In *The American Dream,* language shapes reality (beige hat, wheat hat, cream hat: same hat), but here language is also used to confuse identity. As close as OTTO and otto are (their mother gave them the same name but used caps and lowercase to differentiate), OTTO still needs "me identically." As in *The Play About the Baby,* need determines reality, and so *otto* (a third person, so italicized) is discovered in OTTO's mirror. While OTTO, otto, and *otto* could be considered the titular characters, "me, myself, and I" is idiomatic for being alone. Here OTTO makes trouble and does terrible things to get away, to be alone, although he claims that *otto* is real. OTTO seeks the power to craft his own identity, and therefore his own existence, free from the influence of his mother and his brother.

I. I Want To Make Trouble (*MMI* 5-38)

In a Pre-Scene "*before the red curtain*," OTTO states his intentions clearly to the audience: "I want to make trouble, because I want to make things even more complicated than they *are* around here, and then maybe I can get rid of this whole mess—this family and everything." When his identical twin brother, otto, enters, OTTO shoves past him and exits, heading for his mother's bedroom. A state of confusion about identity exists even before OTTO makes trouble. Mother asks, "Which one are you? I never know who you are," and "Are you the one who loves me?" Soon after that, OTTO counters, "you never tell me…who I am." Frequent reference is made to the fact that the twins' father left immediately after their birth twenty-eight years ago; resonant with Man's philosophy in *The Play About the Baby*, Father loved Mother "but the glory was too much" (*MMI* 24, cf. 75). Mother's doctor then moved in with her. Even after twenty-eight years of this reality, Mother still refers to him as "my doctor," and Dr. says, "I don't live here" (but then concedes that he does after being corrected by OTTO and Mother). Mother says of their father, "I was his first. I was his only," which recalls Martin's claim of Sylvia being his first and only goat (*3CP* 584). While Mother assumes the boys' father is dead, OTTO believes he will come back. This would be somewhat resonant of Malcolm's hope for his father's return, except that OTTO's claim that his father might return with "sacks of emeralds, panthers in tow" foreshadows an event orchestrated by OTTO that closes the play. As in *The Play About the Baby*, reality and existence are defined with verbal assertions. OTTO says, "I have a *new* brother now. The old one is gone. He doesn't exist," and claims "I've decided I'm going to be Chinese," although this does not deter him and his mother from making callous stereotypical remarks (*MMI* 15, 25, 33; cf. also a reference to Mao, 28).

Dr., who can tell OTTO and otto apart because "Neither one of them loves me" and who is therefore "never confused by affection" and whose function in part is "Delaying chaos," suggests that "everything would have been easier if you hadn't named them both Otto" and asserts, "You strew confusion in your path." The confusion of identity and reality continues with Mother saying "they knew they were the same person" and otto recalling OTTO at age 11 scaring a girl by saying "There's really only one of us." otto says of this girl, "OTTO tried to take her away from me. He said she'd be fun to bounce on." otto's sense of possession and OTTO's disrespect are disturbing, especially given that the comments were made when they were 11 years old. otto's characterization of the person he remembers as simply "fat girl" is also insensitive, as is OTTO's saying that his father must have married his mother "for her breasts alone" (9). All of Albee's character descriptions for this play are more reductive than usual, but the flippant condescension of Maureen's description as "25, pretty, etc." (4) is noteworthy. OTTO's interest in girls otto likes and, upon otto's announcement that he has a girlfriend named Maureen, Mother's "I suppose this means your brother has a girlfriend named Maureen, too" foreshadow OTTO's betrayal in Act Two. Mother is actually wondering whether her sons are dating identical twins, but otto says OTTO'd "never do anything like that, date an identical, that it was hard enough knowing who *he* was." OTTO's "I have a twin brother, but now I have a different one" and "The one I had doesn't *exist* anymore" gels with otto's assertion that OTTO treats him "as if I wasn't there, as if I…didn't exist." This treatment enhances otto's sensitivity to his identity, and he counters his Mother's calling him darling with "I have a name." When Dr. and Mother inform otto that his brother says he's been replaced and that he doesn't exist, otto demands, "I want him to talk to *me*. I want him to tell it to my face." Dr. counters, "If you don't exist, how can he tell you?"

II. You Really Did Terrible Things (*MMI* 39-77)

otto pleads with Maureen to confirm his existence: "You *see* me; you *feel* me." Her emphatic "Yes!!" prompts "Then...I exist." Regarding his brother, otto laments, "He looks right at me...and he doesn't *see* me." otto asks Maureen to talk to his mother and convince her that he's "not some thing they don't believe in." OTTO, who has solicited the audience's silence to spy on this scene, takes a moment to clarify the confusion for those of us who may be "staring off—into the middle distance" (which resonates with Albee's motif of the eyes as a measure of engagement): "My brother *did* exist, but now I need him *not* to" (46, cf. 65). So, as in *The Play About the Baby*, reality is determined by need. OTTO speaks fondly of otto, concluding with an articulation of a dual reality: "we were each other, after all. Ourselves...*and* each other." OTTO stays to spy on the next scene, citing "the tradition that if you lean against a proscenium...the people who are *in* the scene won't see you." Albee may be suggesting that if we accept this theatrical convention that runs counter to our perceptions of reality, then we might also accept the twins' dual identity as the same person and as different persons and accept that otto might not exist even given our sensory perception of him. Albee continues to flaunt theatrical conventions to underscore how we allow our imaginations to craft reality. Mother and Dr. come onstage for a "picnic" that has been arranged in order for them to meet Maureen. Dr. counters Mother's "This looks like a good spot" with "It looks like everywhere else" (all spots in the open downstage area look the same). Mother justifies Dr.'s "I don't like outdoors" with "you can't have a picnic indoors" (but they are indoors onstage). When

Dr. laments not meeting at home, there is this exchange that calls attention to the replacement of Mother's bedroom with the twins' bedrooms
during intermission:

> Mother: (*Looks about her; impatient.*) Do you see it? Do you
> see the bedroom? Do you see the room anywhere?
> Dr.: (*Looking.*) No. Where is it, by the way?
> Mother: (*Indicating stage right.*) Off there somewhere.
> Certainly not here.
> Dr.: Things just…vanish around this place. (49)

Although there is no stage direction asking for sound effects, Mother
says, "Do you hear birds? *I* do."

Albee highlights how meaning and even existence can be ambiguous
given that our realities are susceptible to our subjective needs and fears.
Mother says, "What people say and what they mean don't always mesh."
Maureen articulates a range of things that being Irish can mean (54-5).
Mother says, "I don't think existence determines much of anything."
Mother sees Maureen as a potential threat and uses language resonant
of Stevie in *The Goat*: "whatever hurts either of my babies, whether they
exist or not, whatever brings them down has my—I almost blush to
say the word—has my wrath. *And* my revenge!" Again, a woman's passionate expression is characterized as performance by her partner (60).
Mother's fear of Maureen presents itself in her prejudiced comments
about Maureen's multiple heritage (55-8). OTTO's next trouble-making
move is to "fuck Maureen," asserting that "She can't tell us apart" but
then wondering "Maybe she *knows*!!" (Albee's stage directions indicate
that Maureen can't tell them apart, 39). otto discovers the post-coital
pair but unleashes the pain of his betrayal on innocent Maureen rather

than culpable OTTO, rejecting Maureen's heartfelt attempts at recon-
ciliation. His final rebuff recalls the language Boy and Girl use to avert
dealing with pain in *The Play About the Baby*: "Later...maybe" (71).
otto gathers everyone together by using "*an imaginary bell pull*" that
prompts "*a loud, summoning clang. Again; again; again.*"

   In order to get away, OTTO must be free of otto, but having an
identical brother is an essential part of OTTO's identity that he can't
lose, so he compensates such that "loss is merely change." OTTO
relates how he had avoided touching his mirror image "For fear I
didn't exist" but then realized "it *wasn't* my image I saw there; it was
just like...exactly like me...but it *wasn't* me; it was someone else. It was
me identically; it was my *real* identical twin." OTTO tells otto, "I'm
finally...myself, and you can be...whoever you need to be," referring
to otto as "my twin, perhaps, but not my brother." As the play builds to
its conclusion, there are numerous examples of reality being decided,
imagined, or denied for one's self or for others. OTTO says to otto,
"Shall I pretend you're here? Shall I pretend you're you?" and of the
baby that may come of OTTO's betrayal, "Let's pretend it's yours." Of
OTTO's denial that otto is his brother, otto chides, "*all* of you...*accept*
this?" otto's quiet response to OTTO's "Is there nothing *left*? Is it all
gone between us?" is "I would *imagine* so." When they embrace to "see
if we can feel anything," otto feels "Something, I think," but OTTO says
"We'd better not admit it." As OTTO prepares to leave, Dr. quips, "Don't
forget your mirror," and Father (so called in the stage directions, but
his spoken line is attributed to Man) arrives with emeralds on a chariot
pulled by black panthers, all fake according to the stage directions, and
a real banner announcing a happy ending. When OTTO, referring to
his twin-but-not-his-brother as "bro," confirms that he brought their
father back, Mother says, "He didn't just...*appear*?" and launches into

a tirade against Father that the others attempt to quell. OTTO decides "You've really fucked it up, Ma" and says, "Sorry, Dad," this prompt seemingly more responsible for Father's exit than Mother's tirade. Therefore, there is an odd logic to OTTO's assertion: "She'll never forgive me for what she did!" OTTO justifies the trouble he makes for his family by admitting to otto, "I just thought if I behaved bad enough you all wouldn't mind my going so much. I just had to get away. I couldn't take it anymore—Ma and all. I just *had* to get out!" OTTO's desire to get away is real, and therefore *otto* (from the mirror) is real, which is why at the end of the play, when OTTO apologizes to otto for telling everyone otto didn't exist, OTTO says of *otto*, "he's real; he *does* exist," and to otto, "I guess we'll just have to think of ourselves as triplets." OTTO's "Well, I think the play's over. Let's go join the curtain call" continues to underscore the theme of contrived reality.

Although OTTO wants to get away from his "perplexing, exhausting, maddening" mother, he also characterizes her as "deeply loving" (61). OTTO speaks of he and otto being "Ourselves...*and* each other" (46), but this intense bond might contribute to OTTO's identity crisis, his aversion, pre-*otto*, to touching his mirror "For fear I didn't exist" (66). OTTO's fear that he doesn't exist influences his need for otto not to exist (46). Fear and loss are always components of reality. Mother's "anticipatory joy" over the impending birth of her boys is accompanied by the potential sorrow that she might lose one or both of them (16). Albee doesn't explore our animal natures in this play, but Dr. assumes animal references relate to their human counterparts—black panthers to Black Panthers (9) and llama to Dalai Lama (13)—before Mother corrects him, confusing differences in spelling with differences in pronunciation (14).

Reality is often a function of language in this play, and Albee's characters' obsessive attention to phrasing and to precision of grammar, meaning, and tense—their "enthusiasm for language" (54)—is more evident in this play (with at least 40 instances) than in any other play in the canon. There are a couple instances of characters admiring each other's wit, too (25, 26-7). OTTO makes several speeches to the audience, and the frequent shift between speaking "in" to characters onstage and "out" to the audience, as in *The Play About the Baby* and *Occupant,* for example, is used here, too. Theatrical conventions are acknowledged by the characters: Dr. says, "We're doing a scene here" (25), and OTTO discusses theatrical traditions (47) and announces intermission (38) and curtain call (77). Albee calls for a red curtain to rise (6) but then to close (38) in the first act. OTTO "*Indicates the curtain*" (77) at the end of the play, but Albee's stage directions call for the upstage areas to darken (76) and relight (77). There is no reference to opening and closing the curtain. *King Lear* is referenced again (22), and Albee has OTTO paraphrase the same passage from novelist James Agee (10) that Mel Gussow used to frame Albee's biography (Gussow 13, 404).

Games are not referenced in this play, but OTTO plays games with the other characters without telling them. There isn't a sense of ritual here, but there are repetitive phrases like "The future's in the East, and I want to be in on it" (first used on 13). There are also instances of *Finding the Sun*'s "you're no help" (10, 15) and *Listening*'s "You're not nice" (17, 50; cf. 61, 71). OTTO has some long speeches, and Mother has a monologue (15-6) in which she acts out both sides of a conversation as in Woman 3's visit to the doctor in *Fragments.* Here, the younger characters have specific names, and the older characters have abstracted names. Fittingly, the environment of this play is abstracted, with "*No naturalistic enclosures*" (6). Although Albee uses blackouts here for scene shifts as he does in his episodic plays, *Me, Myself & I* ends with a climactic event and a partial resolution of plot, and centers around confusion of identity and the use of language to craft reality.

A SUGGESTION FOR STAGING
THE ALBEE CANON

I. The Wheel of Fortune

    A. Nature's Call: *The Sandbox* and *Finding the Sun* in rep with *Seascape*

    B. Twin Destinies: *The American Dream* in rep with *Me, Myself & I*

    C. Fortune's Vicissitudes: *Malcolm* in rep with *The Man Who Had Three Arms* and *Knock! Knock! Who's There!?*

II. Maiden, Matron, Crone

    A. Desire: *Tiny Alice* in rep with *Lolita*

    B. Suffering: *The Death of Bessie Smith* in rep with *All Over*

    C. Release: *Three Tall Women* in rep with *Occupant*

III. Bound to Struggle

    A. Terror and Longing: *A Delicate Balance* in rep with *Marriage Play*

    B. Desperation and Fear: *Everything in the Garden* in rep with *The Lady from Dubuque*

    C. Aggressive Forces: *Box* and *Quotations from Chairman Mao Tse-tung* in rep with *Counting the Ways* and *Listening*

IV. What Cannot Be Undone

A. Lives Without Touching: *At Home at the Zoo* in rep with *Fragments*

B. Taboo Loves: *The Ballad of the Sad Café* in rep with *The Goat, or Who Is Sylvia?*

C. Wounds: *Who's Afraid of Virginia Woolf?* in rep with *The Play About the Baby*

A Suggestion for
Staging the Albee Canon

Longing to live in a world where a theatre company could decide to do all of Shakespeare's histories in a season or the entire August Wilson cycle, I've outlined above a suggestion for staging the Albee canon in a year. More realistically, I hope the outline might inspire a theatre company to commit to presenting Albee shows in repertory once a season, knowing that they could complete the canon in twelve years. I've split the canon (excluding *Fam and Yam*, which Albee did not include in his final collected volumes) into four groups, balanced with one Pulitzer (including Adler's half-Pulitzer, *Virginia Woolf*) and one adaptation per group.

I. The Wheel of Fortune

While it is practical to present Albee's beach plays together—Albee himself has presented *The Sandbox* and *Finding the Sun* together, but with *Box* in the same evening (Solomon 10, Gussow 365) rather than with *Seascape* in rep—there is a thematic resonance of death and rebirth that links the beach plays as well. Also recall the lady from Dubuque's vivid dream about dying that was set "on a beach at sunset" (*2CP* 666-7). Edmee in *Finding the Sun* says "only here, where the earth and water meet, do I feel this…tristesse.…One element into another" (*3CP* 236). Grandma's passing is ceremonious, while Henden's is unexpected. These natural deaths are contrasted with Abigail's unnatural suicide attempt. Fergus presumably leaves the beach to better affect his evolution into an adult. In *Seascape*, Nancy urges Charlie's figurative rebirth from his closed down state, and they both offer to help Leslie and Sarah with their evolutionary rebirth. The family of *The Sandbox* returns in *The American Dream* to enact Grandma's move from one element into another in a different way. The fortunes of the Young Man—Grandma's angel of death in *The Sandbox*, now the American Dream—are inextricably linked with the twin he never knew. OTTO in *Me, Myself & I* attempts to escape his twin, otto, in a quest for unique identity. Malcolm's fortunes fluctuate as he is led by Cox to those who are shown the abyss by the glory of his innocence, but Malcolm's inherent innocence leads him to a pure death rather than a corrupted life. Himself, the man who had three arms, laments his change of fortune, but experiences a rebirth of sorts at the close of his play. The critic in *Knock! Knock! Who's There!?* believes passionately that he belongs at the performance, but fortune has placed him behind a boarded-up door. It's also fitting to play *Knock! Knock! Who's There!?* in repertory with two of Albee's most critically ill-received plays. Albee's critical fortunes would experience a rebirth shortly after *The Man Who Had Three Arms* and *Finding the Sun* with *Three Tall Women*.

II. Maiden, Matron, Crone

Miss Alice, a maiden who first meets Julian disguised as a crone, tempts Julian to succumb to his desires. Lolita, sexually experienced at a young age, tempts Humbert into their first union (the stage directions in *Lolita* specifically referencing *Tiny Alice*, 3CP 66), but she resents Humbert's kidnapping her and forcing her to suffer the expression of his odd, obsessive desires. Self-concern fuels these desires. Julian's inability to deny his subjective self is an obstacle to his faith, and Humbert is a pathological narcissist. The Wife in *All Over* realizes in the end that "All we've *done* is think about ourselves" (*2CP* 366), but her suffering over her husband's retreat from her (The Best Friend's wife suffers from his retreat of her as well) does not keep her from retreating from her children, which fuels their suffering. Father, Nurse, Intern, Orderly, and Jack in *The Death of Bessie Smith* all suffer from a lack of agency. The wisdom of The Wife's epiphany did not prompt release from suffering; often only death prompts this release, and only impending death prompts the wisdom of self-reflection. The dying woman of *Three Tall Women* reflects upon the stages of her life all at once—maiden C, matron B, crone A—and another tall woman (*3CP* 645), Nevelson in *Occupant*, makes a posthumous account of the stages of hers.

III. Bound to Struggle

In *A Delicate Balance*, Agnes and Tobias struggle to honor the obligations of friendship when Henry and Edna, struggling with their terror, come to stay with them. In *Marriage Play*, Jack and Gillian struggle with the obligations of a thirty-year marriage, and Jack also struggles with the effect of routine on his identity. Even in the early days of their marriage, Gillian notes "the terror and longing in his eyes when he is on me" (*3CP* 271). Both *Everything in the Garden* and *The Lady from Dubuque* feature the friendships of multiple couples, friends who struggle with their fear of exclusion, prompting a desperation that leads to bad choices. In *Garden*, inclusion is equated with satisfying petty, materialistic desires. Making bad choices to obtain the money to satisfy those desires exacerbates the characters' baseness and self-absorption. In *Dubuque*, conversation devolves into meanness born of personal insecurities, and Sam's fear of losing Jo makes him so desperate that she must be rescued by angels of death. Presenting Albee's most experimental plays together highlights our struggle with aggressive forces: *Box* laments the inevitability with which obstacles to our potential arise; *Quotations from Chairman Mao Tse-tung* examines the intensity with which we define and resist reality; *Counting the Ways* explores how civilized thought puts us at a distance from the visceral reality of animal instinct; and *Listening* reveals how menace can be calmly effected and coldly distant.

IV. What Cannot Be Undone

Jerry in *At Home at the Zoo* laments that "We neither love nor hurt because we do not try to reach each other" (*AHZ* 40), but the intensity of the love or hurt we might experience, the glory that might show us the abyss, cannot be undone and makes us hesitate. Peter's college experience of hurting someone in a sexual act influences his sexual hesitance with his wife, Ann, who hesitates to reach out to Peter for fear he won't reach back. Jerry, frustrated by his inability to reach others, forces life-altering contact with Peter. Resonant with Jerry's lament, Man 4 in *Fragments* wonders "why we all go through our lives without touching one another very much" (*3CP* 455). This prompts a rare instance in the canon of the gap between desire and offer being bridged as the rest of the ensemble reach for and touch Man 4. Significantly, that event could not have occurred if the ensemble had not built trust through mutual, supportive sharing of experience. If Jerry had been less aggressive and Peter more open, the event in the park may have played out differently. Our impulses to reach each other are more successful if there is a foundation of mutual interest, like that established in *Fragments*. In *The Ballad of the Sad Café*, Marvin's reach for Amelia, Amelia's reach for Lymon, and Lymon's reach for Marvin are all one-sided and doomed to be unrequited. Indulging in love that is unrequited or taboo, we risk great loss. In *The Goat, or Who Is Sylvia?*, Martin, in loving a goat, has done "what cannot be undone" (*3CP* 610), irreparably wounding himself and his family. Man in *The Play About the Baby* asks, "Without wounds, what are you?" (*3CP* 534) Man and Woman inflict wounds that cannot be undone on Boy and Girl, resonant with George's game of Get the Guests in *Who's Afraid of Virginia Woolf?* Albee resisted comparison of these plays (*SMM* 289), noting that George and Martha's child never existed, while Boy and Girl's child existed and then did not. But if George's assumptions are correct, Honey was pregnant with a real baby that was then aborted, so both plays feature characters not ready for the pain and loss of having a baby, although in Honey's case this likely has more to do with her fear of Nick's fitness as a father than with the fears associated with a baby. Honey says, "I want a child" (*1CP* 298). Comparing these plays highlights Albee's maturation as a playwright. Like *Woolf*, *Baby* deals with ambiguous identities and problems discerning truth and illusion, but while *Woolf* is mired in the "corruption of weakness and petty revenges" (*1CP* 301), *Baby* tempers the manipulation of the younger couple with an air of elegant, though malicious, mystery. Addressing the audience in *Baby* also broadens its scope, giving it a more universal quality, and *Baby* goes further than *Woolf* in getting at the root cause of problems discerning truth and illusion, problems that derive from privileging need over stark reality.

THERE ARE OASES

Two hours after any session begins all the relations between
the people present are slightly modified, because of the
experience in which they have been plunged together. As a
result, something is more animated, something flows more
freely, some embryonic contacts are being made between
previously sealed-off souls. When they leave the room,
they are not quite the same as when they entered. If what
has happened has been shatteringly uncomfortable, they
are invigorated to some degree as if there have been great
outbursts of laughter. Neither pessimism nor optimism
apply: simply, some participants are temporarily, slightly,
more alive. If, as they go out of the door, this all evaporates,
it does not matter either. Having had this taste, they will
wish to come back for more. The drama session will seem
an oasis in their lives.

-Peter Brook on "a psychodrama session in an asylum"
from *The Empty Space* (133-4)

Bennett asserts that playwrights of the Absurd go "one step further
than just laughing at our absurd situation" and ask "what do we
do about it?" (Bennett *RTA* 20) So what do we do about the absurd

situation that Albee characterizes so well throughout his body of work: our inability to reach our fellow man, the gap between our desire and what other people can offer us? Esslin suggests that "by facing up to anxiety and despair and the absence of divinely revealed alternatives, anxiety and despair can be overcome" (Esslin 426). Camus, who used the myth of Sisyphus to initiate the idea of the Absurd, said that we "must imagine Sisyphus happy" (Camus 91). Since effort ("Participate, I suppose," *3CP* 456) is the essential response to existence, we can certainly imagine Sisyphus happier than Agnes in *A Delicate Balance*, for whom "There are no mountains in my life…nor chasms. It is a rolling, pleasant land" (*2CP* 23). But Sisyphus is still alone with a rock. What if his situation involved the struggle to reach other people who could never truly understand him? This is our absurd situation, and facing the truth of it might relieve our anxiety, but some despair over being misunderstood will always be with us. Clare Hayes-Brady, though—writing about David Foster Wallace, whom I've cited a couple of times in this book as a writer who debuted about the same time as Albee's *Marriage Play* and explored territory similar to Albee's—says that misunderstanding actually works against isolation, which is a function of completion or perfection:

> [T]he fundamental impossibility of complete communication—that is to say, an act of communication that enacts perfect expression, and perfect interpretation—which intuitively seems to *reinforce* the threat of solipsistic isolation, actually necessitates the recognition or acknowledgement of an unreachable subjective other. The existence of this untouchable subjectivity is necessitated by the interpretive gap, which exists only because of the inevitably incomplete

nature of communication, and so, counter-intuitively, the necessary failure of communicative exchange functions as proof against solipsistic tragedy. (Hayes-Brady 10)

We make meaning of our lives by facing reality, but our reality—our identity—is continuously shaped and challenged by other people, by unreachable subjective others with whom, as Albee relentlessly reminds us, we are irrevocably intertwined. Albee said of *The Goat* in 2004, "The play is about love, and loss, the limits of our tolerance and who, indeed, we really are" (*SMM* 262). He could have been speaking of any of his plays (cf. Zinman 9). Speaking of *The Goat* again in 2005, he said, "I wanted people to go to that play, and imagine themselves in the situation, and really think hard about how they would respond if it was happening to them" (*SMM* 284). As desiring, self-focused beings, we can't escape the absurdity of our situation, but through awareness and empathy we can at least temper our sense of isolation and despair with moments of discovery and communion and even happiness in those brief intervals at the summit of the hill before our rocks all roll down their separate paths again. Himself in *The Man Who Had Three Arms* says, "Everything *may* be on its way downhill,…but all is not that way: there are oases. But one of the rules of an oasis would seem to be that the surrounding desert stretches beyond conjecture;…the way of the world does *not* give us an excess of oases" (*3CP* 148). But we can occasionally give each other an oasis, although acting on that impulse involves risk. Taking a cue from *Fragments* (risking dismissal) or from *Seascape* (risking danger, cf. *SMM* 287), on our way up or down the hill we could risk putting aside the mechanical routine of pushing or chasing our own rocks to reach out to someone else who is struggling to face the stark reality of theirs.

Works Cited

Edward Albee

    1CP   *The Collected Plays of Edward Albee, Volume 1*

    2CP   *The Collected Plays of Edward Albee, Volume 2*

    3CP   *The Collected Plays of Edward Albee, Volume 3*

    AD/ZS *The American Dream and The Zoo Story*

    AHZ   *At Home at the Zoo*

    FAY   *The Sandbox and The Death of Bessie Smith (with Fam and Yam)*

    MMI   *Me, Myself & I*

    SMM   *Stretching My Mind*

Michael Y. Bennett

    EAA   *Edward Albee and Absurdism*

    RTA   *Reassessing the Theatre of the Absurd*

David Foster Wallace
>   OB   *Oblivion*
>
>   TIW   *This Is Water*
>
>   TPK   *The Pale King*

Adler, Thomas P. "Albee's 3½: The Pulitzer Plays" in *The Cambridge Companion to Edward Albee*. Ed. Stephen Bottoms. Cambridge University Press, 2005.

Albee, Edward. *The American Dream and The Zoo Story*. New York: Plume, 1997.

Albee, Edward. *At Home at the Zoo*. New York: Dramatist's Play Service, Inc., 2008.

Albee, Edward. *The Collected Plays of Edward Albee*, 3 vols. New York: Overlook Duckworth, 2004-5.

Albee, Edward. *Me, Myself & I*. New York: Dramatist's Play Service, Inc., 2011.

Albee, Edward. *The Sandbox and The Death of Bessie Smith (with Fam and Yam)*. New York: Plume, 1988.

Albee, Edward. *Stretching My Mind*. New York: Carroll & Graf Publishers, 2005.

Beckett, Samuel. *The Unnamable* in *Samuel Beckett: The Grove Centenary Edition*, Vol. 2. New York: Grove Press, 2006.

Beckett, Samuel. *Waiting for Godot* in *Samuel Beckett: The Grove Centenary Edition*, Vol. 3. New York: Grove Press, 2006. (Albee wrote the introduction to this volume.)

Bennett, Michael Y., editor. *Edward Albee and Absurdism*. Leiden: Brill, 2017.

Bennett, Michael Y. *Reassessing the Theatre of the Absurd*. New York: Palgrave Macmillan, 2011.

Brook, Peter. *The Empty Space*. New York: Touchstone (Simon & Schuster), 1968.

Camus, Albert. *The Myth of Sisyphus and Other Essays*. New York: Vintage, 1955.

Esslin, Martin. *The Theatre of the Absurd*, 3rd ed. New York: Vintage, 2004.

Grant, Paul Benedict. "'A wet run, so to speak': Sex and Sexuality in Edward Albee's Lolita" in *Sex, Gender, and Sexualities in Edward Albee's Plays*. Eds. John M. Clum and Cormac O'Brien. Leiden: Brill, 2018.

Gussow, Mel. *Edward Albee: A Singular Journey*. New York: Simon & Schuster, 1999.

Hayes-Brady, Clare. *The Unspeakable Failures of David Foster Wallace*. New York: Bloomsbury, 2016.

Jenckes, Norma. "Postmodernist Tensions in Albee's Recent Plays" in *Edward Albee: A Casebook*. Ed. Bruce J. Mann. New York: Routledge, 2003.

Lefkowitz, David. "Albee's *Gide* Exiled at OB's Signature as Bancroft *Occupant* Arrives, Feb. 5-March 17." *Playbill*, 6 Dec. 2001, http://www.playbill.com/article/albees-gide-exiled-at-obs-signature-as-bancroft-occupant-arrives-feb-5-march-17-com-100164

Marcia, David. "'The Aims of Spirit': Performing Marriage in Albee's Plays" in *Sex, Gender, and Sexualities in Edward Albee's Plays*. Eds. John M. Clum and Cormac O'Brien. Leiden: Brill, 2018.

Miller, Arthur. *Death of a Salesman* in *The Penguin Arthur Miller*. New York: Penguin, 2015.

Pease, Donald E. "Malcolm, Sexual Politics, Edward Albee's Adaptations" in *Sex, Gender, and Sexualities in Edward Albee's Plays*. Eds. John M. Clum and Cormac O'Brien. Leiden: Brill, 2018.

Roudané, Matthew. *Edward Albee: A Critical Introduction*. Cambridge: Cambridge University Press, 2017.

Solomon, Rakesh. *Albee in Performance*. Bloomington: Indiana University Press, 2010.

Wallace, David Foster. *Oblivion*. Boston: Little, Brown, 2004.

Wallace, David Foster. *The Pale King*. Boston: Little, Brown, 2011.

Wallace, David Foster. *This Is Water*. Boston: Little, Brown, 2009.

Wallach, Eric. "Interview, or Who's Afraid of Mr. Albee?" *The Brooklyn Rail*, 1 Apr. 2005, http://brooklynrail.org/2005/04/theater/albee-interview

Zinman, Toby. *Edward Albee*. Ann Arbor: University of Michigan Press, 2008.